MARTIN PULLEN is a BAFTA director of many children's Paddington Bear, The Wombles passion for trivia, he has now written and illustrated his first book, *The Completely Useless Guide to Christmas*.

MARTIN PULLEN

JOHN BLAKE

Published by John Blake Publishing Ltd
3 Bramber Court, 2 Bramber Road,
London W14 9PB, England

www.johnblakepublishing.co.uk

www.facebook.com/Johnblakepub   facebook

twitter.com/johnblakepub   twitter

First published in paperback in 2013

ISBN: 978 1 78219 477 4

British Library Cataloguing-in-Publication Data:

A catalogue record for this book is available from the British Library.

Design by www.envydesign.co.uk

Printed in Great Britain by CPI Group (UK) Ltd, Croydon CR0 4YY

1 3 5 7 9 10 8 6 4 2

Papers used by John Blake Publishing are natural, recyclable products
made from wood grown in sustainable forests. The manufacturing processes
conform to the environmental regulations of the country of origin.

Every attempt has been made to contact the relevant copyright-holders,
but some were unobtainable. We would be grateful if the appropriate
people could contact us.

FOR DOREEN

Contrary to popular belief, it is not disrespectful to abbreviate Christmas to Xmas. The X represents the Greek letter *chi*, the first letter of *Christos*, meaning Christ. Xmas has been in use since the sixteenth century.

CONTENTS

Section 1

HERE COMES
SANTA CLAUS

Chapter 1

LITTLE SAINT NICK

ST NICHOLAS, known throughout much of the world as Santa Claus, is, amongst many other things, the patron saint of children, merchants, archers, sailors and thieves.

He first became popular in America in the eighteenth century, having arrived from Europe along with the Dutch; the Dutch name for St Nicholas, *Sinterklaas*, over time becoming Santa Claus.

At first dressed in green, wearing a broad-brimmed hat, a huge pair of Flemish ballooned breeches and smoking a long pipe...

...Santa later evolved into the image of a joker, with red waistcoat, yellow stockings and a blue three-cornered hat – a colour combination well-deserving of a visit from the fashion police.

The present-day image of Santa Claus is thought to have partly come from Clement Clarke Moore, an Episcopal Church minister who, in his poem, *An Account of a Visit from St Nicholas*, described a portly figure who flew from house to house on Christmas Eve in a sleigh pulled by eight reindeer.

Squeezing down chimneys, St Nicholas would leave presents for children, but only if they had been well behaved.

In 1881, caricaturist and political cartoonist Thomas Nast, believed to be the creator of the all-American 'Uncle Sam' image, gave Santa a bushy white beard, pot belly and red clothes.

3

With Santa already dressed in the colours of their logo, in 1931 Coca-Cola commissioned artist Haddon Sundblom to illustrate Santa Claus drinking a bottle of the fizzy beverage for their Christmas advertising campaign.

Although Sundblom's illustrations finally gave us the image most popular today, the claim that this image of Santa was created by Coca-Cola is, in reality, little more than successful advertising.

Sinterklaas

Saint Nicholas, good holy man!
Put on the Tabard, best you can;
Go, therewith, to Amsterdam.

Christmas comes early in the Netherlands and many other European countries. Having spent the year noting the behaviour of children in his special red book, Sinterklaas, dressed in Bishop's robes, sets sail from Spain by steamboat, arriving mid-November at Amsterdam docks.

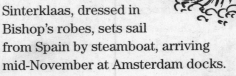

Accompanying Sinterklaas on his journey is his band of 'Black Peter' helpers. The story goes that St Nicholas was at a market in the ancient city of Myra when he saw an Ethiopian boy being sold for slavery. He freed the boy and, in return, the youngster decided to stay with him as his helper. Depicted dressed as a Spaniard, with a feathered cap, black curly hair and a blackened face, the image of 'Black Peter' is no longer considered politically correct, and the modern story tells that Black Peter has a blackened face because he has had to climb down sooty chimneys to deliver the children's presents.

Having disembarked from Amsterdam's docks, Sinterklaas leads a parade through the streets on his white horse, Amerigo. Meanwhile, his helpers throw sweets to well-behaved children, a tradition said to come from the saving of three young girls from prostitution by the tossing of gold coins through their window at night to pay for their father's debts.

Whilst children deemed badly behaved face the bristly end of Black Peter's chimney sweep's brush...

…really naughty children risk being bundled into Sinterklaas's sack and carted back to Spain!

Santa having arrived early, St Nicholas is celebrated on 5 December, St Nicholas Eve, with the exchange of presents. The following day is St Nicholas Day, and that's it, festivities over for another year.

For country folk, this early end could well be a blessing in disguise as, continuing a tradition announcing the birth of the baby Jesus, every evening at sunset for the entirety of Christmas, farmers in the Netherlands blow long wooden horns.

And just to make sure their signal does not go unheeded, they amplify the sound by blowing the horns over water wells.

Klausjagen

In Switzerland, the arrival of St Nicholas is celebrated in the village of Küssnacht with the Klausjagen (St Nicholas chase) Festival.

On the evening of 5 December, following the firing of a cannon, a procession sets off, led by men cracking long sheep whips.

Close behind, white-robed celebrants called 'lifeltrager' pass through the streets wearing illuminated lanterns on their heads. Up to two metres in height, the lanterns resemble a cross between a bishop's mitre and a stained-glass window.

The lightheaded lifeltrager are followed by St Nicholas, his four 'Schmutzli' helpers in black robes, torchbearers, a brass band playing traditional Christmas songs, 700 cowbell ringers and a further 180 men blowing long cow horns.

The parade continues until 7am the following morning, St Nicholas Day. By all accounts, time to invest in a decent pair of earplugs!

Krampus

Sounding not unlike a muscle pain acquired on a German camping holiday, Krampus is considered to be St Nicholas's evil twin, accompanying him on his travels, delivering Christmas presents to the children of Austria and other Alpine countries. When the horned and monstrous-tongued goat-like creature finds what it considers to be a very badly behaved child, it lures the youngster to its underground lair, later to feast on it for Christmas dinner.

Increasingly celebrated in other European countries and parts of the United States, on 5 December, Krampus Night, men bearing torches and dressed in hairy goat-like costumes pass through the streets of towns and villages, frightening and punishing children who have misbehaved. Only this time, the good ones don't get sweets...

Chapter 2

SANTA CLAUS IS COMING TO TOWN

EACH year, Santa Claus visits the Royal Navy Submarine Museum in Gosport, Hampshire, giving out presents to followers of the Christian faith from his grotto inside a Second World War submarine.

Whether squeezing down the hatch of a submarine, or coming down the chimney, Santa arrives in many ways. And he's not always a portly figure with a bushy beard...

Bosnia
The children of Bosnia receive their presents from Grandfather Frost.

California
In the US state of California, Santa Claus arrives on a surfboard.

9

China
Christmas presents are delivered to children in China by Dun Che Lao Ren, the Christmas Old Man.

Hawaii
On the island of Hawaii, Santa Claus arrives by canoe.

Japan
In Japan, children receive their presents from a Buddhist monk by the name of Hotei-osho. Hotei-osho is said to have eyes in the back of his head, and can see if children misbehave.

Syria

The children of Syria receive gifts from one of the Wise Men's camels. The camel is thought to have been the smallest one in the Wise Men's caravan.

Ukraine

Whilst the children of the Ukraine sleep, they are visited by Father Frost, travelling in a sleigh pulled by three reindeer.

Father Frost is joined on his travels by the Snowflake Girl, who wears a snowflake-shaped crown and a blue costume with white fur trim.

Section 2

CHRISTMAS TRIMMINGS

Chapter 3

WE THREE KINGS OF ORIENT ARE

THERE is no mention of *three* wise men in the Bible. There is also no mention of a cat. But there is, however, mention of a car: it says that Moses came down the mountain in his Triumph. They say the old jokes are the best.

The Gospel of Matthew states that 'wise men came from the East' to visit the newly born baby Jesus. Although the Bible fails to record how many they were, it has been assumed there were three as they brought with them three gifts: gold, frankincense and myrrh.

Gold

Around 2600 BC, the Egyptian King Tushratta claimed that gold was more common than earth. In a land of sand, the King may well have been right.

With the metal in abundance, the Aztecs described gold as 'the excrement of the gods', placing more value on feathers and turquoise.

Since the ancient Egyptians wrote of gold in their hieroglyphs, around 168,000 tonnes of the precious metal have been mined – enough gold bars to build a second Great Pyramid of Giza.

Rolled out with a giant rolling pin, this would be enough gold leaf to cover the entire British Isles.

The amount of new gold mined each year would just about fill a double-decker bus or – rolled into gold leaf – cover the county of Norfolk.

During the fourteenth century, drinking molten gold and crushed emeralds was used as a treatment for bubonic plague.

A number of Native American tribes thought eating gold would give them the ability to levitate.

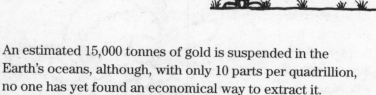

An estimated 15,000 tonnes of gold is suspended in the Earth's oceans, although, with only 10 parts per quadrillion, no one has yet found an economical way to extract it.

Resistant to corrosion, alloyed with copper or silver, gold is well suited for use in coins. The Romans minted their coins in the temple of Juno Moneta, in the hills of Rome. It was from Juno Moneta that we get the word 'money'.

Frankincense

A sweet-smelling gum resin, frankincense begins as a thick milky sap, extracted from the *Boswellia sacra*, a tough old boot of a tree that survives in the dry and rocky soil of Oman and Somalia. To say it survives may be putting it strongly, as recent studies have shown that the population of the tree is in decline, due to a combination of over-tapping, cattle grazing and attacks by the longhorn beetle.

Once worth its weight in gold, frankincense could again prove invaluable, as studies are being carried out into the long-term effects of its use in the treatment of inflammatory bowel diseases.

Were you to be spending Christmas in a hot, wet climate, burning frankincense will keep mosquitoes at arm's length, in turn lowering the chances of contracting malaria.

In ancient times, frankincense enemas were used to treat leprosy.

The Egyptians burned frankincense and ground the remains into a powder, which they used as black eyeliner.

Mostly now used in perfumery and aromatherapy, frankincense scent is thought to represent life, a fitting gift for the baby Jesus.

Myrrh

According to Greek mythology, Myrrha fell in love with her father, fooling him into an incestuous relationship. To save her from her father's rage, the gods turned her into a tree – the myrrh tree – where she shed tears of myrrh.

With its roots on somewhat firmer ground, myrrh is the congealed gum resin from the *Commiphora guidottii* tree, widely found in Somalia and eastern parts of Ethiopia.

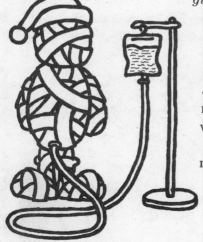

The third of the Wise Men of the East's gifts to the baby Jesus, at the time of the newborn king's birth, myrrh was as valuable as gold.

Ancient Egyptians used myrrh in the embalming of mummies.

As well as being used to relieve rheumatism, arthritis, haemorrhoids and menopausal pain, in Chinese medicine myrrh is thought to have beneficial effects on the invisible meridian channels to the heart, liver and spleen.

In modern medicine myrrh is used to treat tonsillitis, gum disease and sore throats, and is found in antiseptic mouthwashes and toothpastes, soaps, lip balms and many cosmetics.

Most popular in perfumes and as incense, you may well find some myrrh in your Christmas stocking.

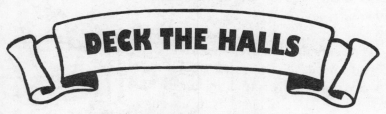

Chapter 4

DECK THE HALLS

The holly and the ivy; and the
mistletoe, and the...

Holly

The Romans were the first to bring
holly into their homes, the spiky leaves
hanging around the fireplace to offer
protection from evil spirits entering
through the chimney.

The tradition passed on to the
Christian church, in time holly leaves
coming to symbolise the crown of thorns
worn by Jesus on the cross, with the red
berries representing Christ's blood.

Before turnips were
introduced into Britain
in the eighteenth
century, the evergreen
holly was grown to feed
cattle and sheep during
the winter months.

Aside from providing a hearty winter meal, the leaves of the Amazonian *Ilex guayusa* holly tree are used to make ayahuasca, a stimulating herbal tea.

If you care to relax over your afternoon tea with a game, the heavy, hard and whitish wood of the holly is traditionally used to make the white chess pieces, taking battle against their ebony opponents.

And, if you were to expire after the Christmas feast, holly provides the perfect wreath.

Ivy

Together with a concoction involving opium and wild lettuce, ivy features in one of the earliest recorded medical formulas for what was known as a 'soporific sponge'. Used as early as the twelfth century as an anaesthetic, the sponge, soaked in the liquefied plant's juices, would be placed over the patient's nose and mouth, inducing up to four days of sleep.

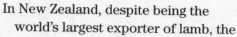

In New Zealand, despite being the world's largest exporter of lamb, the fluffy balls of wool-covered meat have never so much as seen a leaf of ivy. Not being native to the country, and with worries that, if introduced, it might spread like an out-of-control bushfire, ivy is banned, excepting, that is, in its depiction on Christmas cards.

Mistletoe

The Anglo-Saxons referred to mistletoe as 'dung on a twig'. They had good reason: the mistle thrush feasts on mistletoe berries, then excretes the seeds in its droppings. Coated with a gluey substance called viscin, the seeds stick to the branches of trees, the viscin hardening. The mistletoe then grows from the bird's droppings, using the faeces as food.

Left unchecked, the mistletoe saps the host tree of water and nutrients, reducing its growth and – with heavy infestation – eventually kills the tree.

With a particular liking for apple trees, and with apples increasingly imported from northern France, orchards in Britain's 'cider counties' of Kent and Somerset are in decline, and British mistletoe, losing its host trees, is facing an uncertain future.

In 2011, the National Trust launched a campaign – fittingly called 'Giving Mistletoe the Kiss of Life' – to preserve British mistletoe. As part of the campaign, the Trust highlighted six different insects that rely on mistletoe for food…

…including the mistletoe marble moth…

…and the romantically-named 'kiss-me-slow' weevil.

According to custom, a young man has the privilege of kissing a girl under hanging mistletoe, although he must then remove a berry. When all the berries have been removed, the privilege ceases. Even if berries remain, the mistletoe must either be burned on the Twelfth Night or, some believe, fed to a cow.

If a man were to kiss under the mistletoe after the Twelfth Night, it's said he won't find love in the coming year.

Poinsettia

In December 1828, on a visit to the Mexican city of Taxco, Doctor Joel Roberts Poinsett, first US Minister to Mexico, discovered a large plant with flame-red, leaf-like bracts, growing by the side of the road. A keen botanist, Poinsett sent a cutting home to be planted in his greenhouse in Greenville, South Carolina.

Dismissed at first by fellow botanists as a weed, following successful cultivation over 65 million poinsettias are now sold each year in the US alone, one-third of annual flowering potted-plant sales.

But is it a pot plant? Left to grow wild, the poinsettia can reach a lofty four metres.

The chameleon of the plant world, in the long dark of the winter night the flame-red bracts change colour. But don't sneak in with your torch to watch – unless it gets a full 12 hours of darkness, a poinsettia will be nothing but grumpy in the morning.

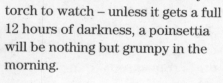

Native to Mexico and Central America, the poinsettia is known locally as *Flor de Nochebuena*, meaning 'Christmas Eve flower'.

Christmas Rose

Story tells of a cold and wintry night, when the Wise Men of the East, on their way to Bethlehem bearing gifts for the newly born baby Jesus, came across a shepherdess by the name of Madelon. Poor Madelon, she was unable to afford – or even find – a small gift, not even a flower, to give the Holy Child! A tear began to run down her cheek. Seeing her weep, an angel swept away the snow to reveal a beautiful white flower: the Christmas rose.

Otherwise known as the Snow or Winter rose, the Christmas rose is often thought of as the true Christmas flower, blooming in the cold of winter in the mountainous Alpine regions of central Europe.

If you're looking for a name at Christmas for your newborn baby girl, perhaps you should forget Holly and go for Madelon – the Christmas rose.

Christmas Cactus

Sounding not unlike a well-sprung mattress, the Schlumbergera is commonly referred to as the Christmas cactus, as – surprise, surprise – it blooms at Christmas. Well, not always: it has been known to flower as early as October, or as late as the following summer.

With a liking for the shade of trees or rocks in areas with high humidity, the Christmas cactus can be found growing wild in the coastal mountain rainforests of southeast Brazil, or in the greenhouse of your local garden centre. It's best to visit near to Christmas Eve and seek out one already in bloom; otherwise, don't hold your breath.

Glastonbury Thorn

Legend tells, after the death of Jesus, Joseph of Arimathea travelled to Britain, bringing with him the Holy Grail. Intending to spread the message of Christianity, Joseph travelled to the West Country, to the town of Glastonbury, where, pushing his walking stick into the ground beside him, he lay down to sleep. Upon awakening, he found the stick had taken root, and begun to flower. Joseph left his walking stick in the ground and, from that day, the Glastonbury thorn – unlike the common single-flowering hawthorn tree – magically blossomed every winter and spring.

It is said that during the English Civil War of 1642–51 the original tree that grew from the walking stick of Joseph of Arimathea

25

was cut down and destroyed by soldiers faithful to Oliver Cromwell; but not before secret cuttings had been taken and planted to grow further trees. One of the trees could be found, until its death in 1984, growing in the grounds of Glastonbury Abbey.

To this day, two other Glastonbury thorns grow in the grounds of the Church of St John the Baptist. From one of these 'sacred thorns', a flowering sprig is sent, every Christmas, to the British monarch, a tradition dating back to the early seventeenth century.

Chapter 5

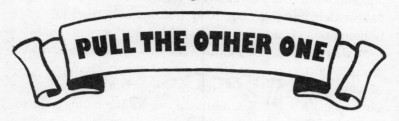

PULL THE OTHER ONE

IN 1840, whilst visiting Paris, Thomas J. Smith, a baker of wedding cakes from London, came across sugared-almond sweets wrapped individually in small squares of waxed paper. Returning home, Smith began selling these French 'bon bons' from his shop in Goswell Road, Clerkenwell.

With the sweets popular with his female clientele, and further inspired by Chinese fortune cookies, Smith began slipping love mottos inside the sweets' wrappings. As popular as the bonbons were, sales dropped off after Christmas, and so, the following year, he wrapped the sweets and motto in a small tube, including either a charm or trinket.

Further encouraged by the crackle of a log fire, Smith then increased the size of the tube, and added two strips of thin card coated with saltpetre. Commonly found in gunpowder, the saltpetre created a small bang when the strips of card were pulled. Eventually the bonbon sweet was replaced with a small gift and, in 1860, Tom Smith's 'Bangs of Expectation' were launched: the Christmas cracker was born.

By 1900, Tom Smith's factory was thought to be selling over 13 million crackers a year.

With Smith long passed on, in 1963 the company moved to Norwich, where it continued to make more than 40 million crackers a year; placed end-to-end, long enough to form a ring around the moon.

No longer just for the ladies, aside from a joke and a paper hat, this is what you might expect to find inside a box of crackers:

Miniature Spyglass
Pretend you are Inspector Clouseau with a miniature spyglass. If your eyesight is going, perfect for reading the joke that came with it.

Miniature Compass
...that permanently points North-North-West!

Plastic ring
With this plastic ring, I thee wed.

Miniature playing cards
Anyone for gin rummy?

Miniature screwdriver
For those holiday DIY jobs!

Curly fish
Read the fortune of every person around the table with a thin red curly fish.

Miniature Shoe Horn
Perfect, if you happen to be one of the seven dwarfs.

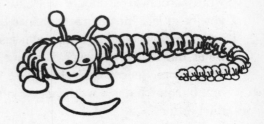

Chapter 6

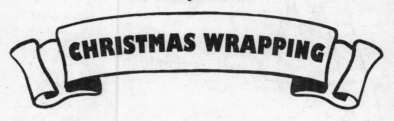

CHRISTMAS WRAPPING

FROM cellulose-based, pressure sensitive adhesive tape, to a two-metre-wide roll of turkey foil: all you need to see you through Christmas...

Sellotape

Apply rubber resin to a cellophane film, change the 'C' to 'S', wrap it around a cardboard tube and slice it into rolls, and what you have is Sellotape, a 'cellulose-based, pressure-sensitive adhesive tape' that has become an essential part of Christmas.

Just like Aspirin, Hoover, Thermos, Escalator, Yo-Yo and many more, Sellotape has become a generic trademark – a brand name that is now the general, known description of the product.

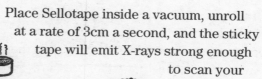

Place Sellotape inside a vacuum, unroll at a rate of 3cm a second, and the sticky tape will emit X-rays strong enough to scan your finger.

With it estimated that every household in the United Kingdom has two rolls of 'pressure-sensitive adhesive tape' tucked away in a drawer at any given time, and, with around 66 metres of tape on an average roll, the UK alone owns enough sticky tape to circle the planet at least 85 times; interestingly, by the thickness of a single roll of tape.

Add all of the tape tucked away in the drawers of the rest of the world, and the Earth could be insulated in a layer of sticky-tape so thick, all thoughts of global warming would be a thing of the past.

Blu Tack

If you don't wish to use a cellulose-based, pressure-sensitive adhesive tape, then there is always 'reusable putty-like pressure-sensitive adhesive'.

Not quite sticking to the brief, the story tells, in 1970, whilst working for a sealant manufacturing company in the Hampshire town of Waterlooville, laboratory researcher Alan Holloway produced a pliable, semi-elastic sealant. The problem was that it didn't seal, although it did just about stick.

At first treated as a novelty, glue manufacturer Bostik became involved and – adding the colour blue to the original white so that children wouldn't mistake it for an edible sweet – they launched Blu Tack.

Now joined by Tack-it, Pritt-Tack, Ticky Tack, Sticky Tack, Tac 'N Stick, White Tack and other tacky rivals, despite it being reusable, there may well be enough new 'reusable putty-like pressure-sensitive adhesive' manufactured each year to make a sticky ball the size of a small planet.

Tinsel

Invented in the German town of
Nuremberg in 1610, tinsel was
originally made of shredded 'fool's
gold' silver, with lead added to give it
weight. By the early twentieth century
the expensive and fragile Christmas
tree decoration had been replaced
by cheaper, aluminium-based tinsel.
Where shredded silver lost its sparkle,
the aluminium proved flammable next
to the hot Christmas lights.

No more lead poisoning or
impromptu indoor firework displays,
as tinsel is now made of PVC.

Gold Marker Pen

One gold marker pen contains enough ink to draw a line at
least 60 metres long, or write 95 Christmas cards, including
their envelopes.

With it estimated that each person
in the UK sends, on average, 31
Christmas cards, one marker pen
should last for around three yea

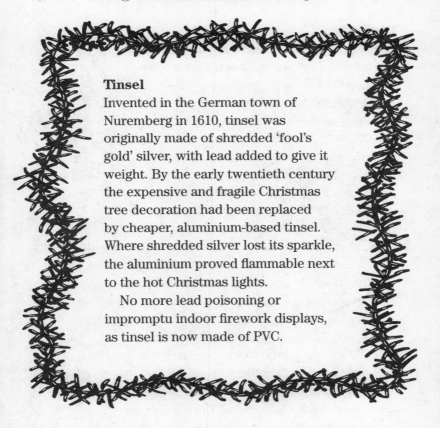

Candles

Whether lit in church for worship, or a Santa Claus table decoration, candles are a must at Christmas.

In the sixteenth century, candles were popularly made of tallow, the smelly fat of a sheep or cow.

Although more expensive, spermaceti – a type of wax found in the head cavities of a sperm whale – was once popular due to its bright-burning flame.

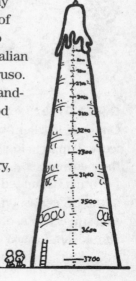

There are many claimants to the crown of the world's biggest candle. In 1921, Ajello Candles created a memorial candle for Italian opera singer and close friend, Enrico Caruso. Decorated with elaborate carvings and hand-painted in oils, the one-tonne candle stood almost 6 metres high and measured 1.5 metres in circumference at the base.

Lit for one day each year on 25 February, the anniversary of Caruso's birth, it is estimated the candle will last for 1,800 years.

The truth will be known in 3721.

Wrapping Paper
Around 30 square miles of wrapping paper is thrown away each Christmas in the UK, enough to cover the Channel Island of Guernsey.

Party Poppers
Although official figures are unavailable, scaled up to the size of a space rocket, it's quite possible the explosive power of a party popper could blast it into orbit.

Batteries
Whether in a camera or the TV remote, a children's toy or grandpa's hearing aid, Christmas would be rather flat without batteries.

Based in Zhangbei, China, electric car manufacturer BYD, working with the State Grid Corporation of China, lays claim to the world's largest battery. Covering more than 10 tennis courts of floor space and with an estimated

weight equivalent of around 300 million
AAA batteries, in the event of a
mains power failure the
giant battery can provide
enough electricity to supply a
community of 12,000 homes for
up to an hour.

On a smaller scale, the most
unusual battery is the electric
eel. With the head acting as a positive pole
and the tail as a negative, a 6-metre eel can
produce enough electricity to run 12 light bulbs.

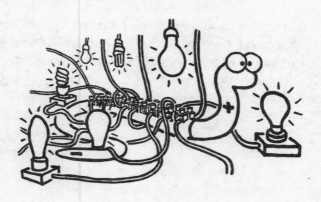

Turkey Foil

Christmas turkey calls – not for the usual
tin foil – but turkey foil, 2 metres wide
and long enough to stretch from
Land's End to John
O'Groats.

Only once does the turkey foil see a turkey; the remaining roll – too wide for the kitchen drawer – finds a home in the broom cupboard, and you spend the next few months, long after the teeth along the edge of the box have worn away, tearing off squares of foil to wrap the kids' school lunches.

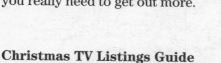

But tin foil is not tin foil; tin foil is aluminium. It was last made of tin during the Second World War, when aluminium not only became cheaper, but was easier to use and didn't leave food tasting of metal.

And if you've ever wondered how thin aluminium foil is, or why one side is shiny and the other matt, then you really need to get out more.

Christmas TV Listings Guide

Oh, the excitement of turning the crisp pages of the Christmas TV listings guide – a literary plume of no less than 280 pages covering 14 days of 'The Best of TV, Film and Radio', from well before Christmas, right through to the New Year – and reading all about your favourite TV soaps, circling everything you plan to watch or record:

…the *Only Fools and Horses* episode where Del Boy falls through the bar…

Morecambe & Wise...

The Great Escape...

If only you could just sit and watch TV all through Christmas...

Chapter 7

THE GREAT ESCAPE

IF ONLY you *could* just sit and watch TV all through Christmas. Time to escape the rush, snuggle under a blanket and relax in front of the TV…

The Wizard of Oz
Toto the dog, munchkins, a cowardly lion, Scarecrow, Tin Man, a pair of ruby slippers and a yellow brick road, the Wicked Witch of the West and five different directors and you have the perennial Christmas favourite, *The Wizard of Oz*.

Twelve-year-old farm girl, Dorothy, is knocked unconscious by a tornado, and along with her dog Toto and the farmhouse, swept up in a storm and deposited in the magical Land of Oz, where she befriends a few social outcasts, sings 'Over the Rainbow' and sets out on the yellow brick road to Emerald City to ask the Wizard of Oz to return her to Kansas.

Based on the novel, *The Wonderful Wizard of Oz*, story tells that the book's author, L. Frank Baum, arrived at the

name of 'Oz' from the letters on the
bottom drawer of his filing cabinet.
Had he chosen the top drawer
we would now all be familiar
with the perennial Christmas
favourite, *The Wizard of An*.

Up against *Gone with the
Wind* at the Oscars, *The
Wizard of Oz* still managed
to win two statuettes, and
has since been named by the
US Library of Congress as the
most-watched film in history.

Life of Brian

Perhaps not a film you would immediately associate with
Christmas, *Life of Brian* does, of course, recount the life
of Jesus.

Well, not exactly Jesus.

Written and directed by the Monty Python
team, the film tells the tale of Brian Cohen,
a young Jewish boy born on the
same day as – and
next door to –
Jesus Christ, a
coincidence
that leads to
him being
mistaken for the
Messiah.

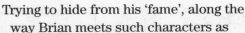

Trying to hide from his 'fame', along the way Brian meets such characters as Judith Iscariot, Naughtius Maximus, Sillius Soddus, Biggus Dickus and the revolutionary group, The People's Front of Judea, The Judean People's Front, The Judean Popular People's Front and The Popular Front of Judea. The film was financed, to the tune of £3 million, by ex-Beatle George Harrison, who co-founded the production company, HandMade Films, after the original backers pulled out at the last minute.

Amongst accusations of blasphemy and protests from religious groups, *Life of Brian* was banned from cinema release in many countries, with New York screenings said to have been picketed by both nuns and rabbis.

Banned by a number of local council authorities in the UK, it wasn't until 2008 – 29 years after its initial release – that Torbay Council in Devon finally allowed the film to be screened. The following year the ban was 'mistakenly' lifted in the Welsh town of Aberystwyth; mistakenly, as it was subsequently discovered the council had never banned the film in the first place.

Despite localised protests, *Life of Brian* enjoyed UK

box-office success, and has since been cited as one of the greatest of comedy films.

Meanwhile, 'Always Look on the Bright Side of Life', sung by fellow crucifixion victims to cheer Brian up whilst left nailed to the cross, reached number three in the UK singles chart, and has since become one of the most requested songs at funerals.

It's a Wonderful Life

In the early days of black and white films, falling snow was created using cornflakes painted white. Being noisy under foot, when it was snowing cornflakes, dialogue in films had to be later added in a voice-dubbing studio. Frank Capra, producer and director of *It's a Wonderful Life*, wanted to record the actors' voices live on set, and so a new snow effect was created using soap and water mixed with the fire-fighting chemical foamite, pumped under pressure through a wind machine.

Capra used over 27,000 litres of the 'silent' snow, and the RKO Effects Department received a Technical Award from the Motion Picture Academy.

Nominated for five Oscars, *It's a Wonderful Life* failed to win a single coveted gold statuette. It also failed at the box office, only growing in popularity after 1974, when an apparent clerical oversight led to Frank Capra's copyright expiring. Passing into the public domain, American television stations were free to air the film repeatedly without paying the director any repeat royalties.

With muppet-creator Jim Henson long gone to the great puppet show in the sky, we'll never know for certain whether he named Bert and Ernie, two of his *Sesame Street* characters, after the policeman and taxi driver in *It's a Wonderful Life*, though it was thought to have been one of his favourite films.

The moving story of George Bailey, dissuaded from committing suicide by guardian angel Clarence Odbody, *It's a Wonderful Life* will melt even the iciest of snowmen.

The Snowman

Talking of snowmen...
Drawn with pastels and
crayons, Raymond Briggs'
illustrated book, brought
to life in animation, tells
the story of a young boy
who, upon waking up and
realising it's snowing, leaps
out of bed, pulls on his
clothes, and bounds outside
to build a snowman.

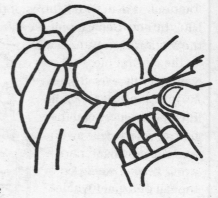

That night, on the stroke of midnight,
the snowman comes to life.
After jumping onto a
motorbike and
attempting to
ride over a few
pheasants and
several other
animals, warm around
the groin area from the
heat of the bike...

...the snowman climbs into
a freezer.

Before long the young boy and the snowman set off on a magical adventure, flying to the North Pole. On the way, they fly over Brighton's Royal Pavilion and Palace Pier, before crossing the ocean, where they swoop past penguins and narrowly avoid getting walloped by the tail of a giant whale.

Reaching the North Pole, the young boy and the snowman watch the northern lights, attend a party of snowmen and meet Santa Claus. Before returning, Santa gives the boy a snowman-pattered scarf.

The next morning, with the sun out, the boy awakes to find the snowman has melted. He begins to wonder whether the night's events were all a dream, until he discovers that he still has the scarf given to him by Santa.

45

A Charlie Brown Christmas

Based upon the comic strip *Peanuts*, by Charles M. Schultz, the animated special, *A Charlie Brown Christmas*, first aired on American TV in 1965 and has, like *The Snowman* in Britain, become a perennial US Christmas favourite.

Getting involved in directing the school nativity, Charlie Brown decides the play would benefit from having a Christmas tree. With friend Linus by his side, he sets off to get a 'big, shiny, aluminium tree'.

At the market, Charlie Brown spots the only remaining real tree and, despite its small and scraggly appearance, he decides that that's the one.

Returning to the nativity, everyone pokes fun at Charlie Brown's choice of tree. Not to be discouraged, he decides to take it home, where he can add decorations and prove their laughter unfounded.

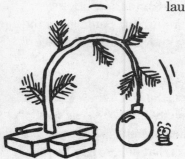

On the way, Charlie Brown and Linus stop at Snoopy's decorated doghouse. After placing a bauble on top of his scraggly tree, the branch flops to one side and, thinking he's killed it, Charlie Brown runs off.

Linus returns to the nativity and informs the others what Charlie Brown has been up to, and they set off for Snoopy's doghouse. Linus wraps the sagging tree in his security blanket, whilst the others place the remainder of Snoopy's decorations on the scraggly branches. Charlie Brown returns, and cannot believe his eyes.

Seen as shunning the over-commercialism of Christmas, in the United States *A Charlie Brown Christmas* has become one of the most beloved animated Christmas specials of all time. To this day, Christmas trees that grow in the wild, with thinner foliage and fewer branches than farmed trees that have been pruned to keep their thickness and shape, are referred to by American Christmas tree farmers as 'Charlie Browns'.

Chapter 8

ROCKIN' AROUND THE CHRISTMAS TREE

ALTHOUGH it is commonly thought to be Prince Albert who introduced the Christmas tree to Britain, it was in fact Queen Charlotte, the German-born wife of King George III, who brought the first tree from her home country to Britain. The tree was displayed for a party in the Queen's Lodge in Windsor in 1800.

Whether the Queen found the time to decorate the tree between giving birth to 14 children is another matter.

Time to put up the Christmas tree…

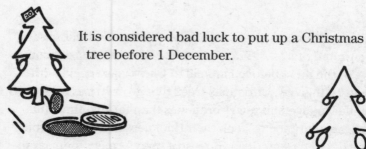

It is considered bad luck to put up a Christmas tree before 1 December.

Taking the tree down before 6 January – the traditional end to Christmas – is also thought to bring bad luck.

It takes between 7 and 10 years for a Christmas tree to reach maturity.

Much of a tree is edible. In particular, pine needles provide a good supply of vitamin C.

A piece of land the size of a football pitch planted with Christmas trees would emit around 40 cubic metres of oxygen a day, enough to supply the needs of 18 people.

In 2011, the Christmas trees in London's Canary Wharf shopping centre displayed round burgundy-coloured tags.

49

Looking not unlike traditional baubles, the tags carried the heart-warming inscription: CCTV in Operation.

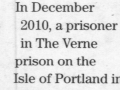

In December 2010, a prisoner in The Verne prison on the Isle of Portland in Dorset was caught growing a 1.2 metre cannabis plant in his cell. According to the local *Dorset Echo* newspaper, the prisoner reportedly tricked the warders by passing the cannabis off as a tomato plant, but the warders became suspicious when he added baubles and tinsel and turned it into a Christmas tree.

According to Ukrainian folklore, a poor widowed mother, unable to afford decorations for her family's Christmas tree, awoke one morning to find the tree beautifully decorated by a spider's web.

And so, in the Ukraine, it is traditional for an artificial spider and web to be hidden in the branches of the Christmas tree, it being said to bring good luck to the person who finds it.

Over Christmas 2010, the Emirates Palace Hotel in Abu Dhabi displayed a 13-metre-tall fake Christmas tree in its lobby, decorated with 131 ornaments encrusted with diamonds, pearls and other precious jewels.

Unfortunately for the Emirates Palace Hotel, it immediately suffered a backlash, the world's media calling the tree, valued at £7 million, ostentatious, in extreme bad taste, and not in the true spirit of Christmas.

Oh dear. Oh very, *very* dear!

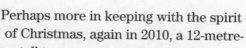

Perhaps more in keeping with the spirit of Christmas, again in 2010, a 12-metre-tall tree was constructed in the Taiwanese city of Taichung, made from 80,000 recycled plastic spoons. The spoons were provided by local branches of fast-food chain, Kentucky Fried Chicken.

Feather Christmas Tree

Environmental concerns regarding deforestation in Germany in the late nineteenth century led to the creation of the feather Christmas tree. The tree was made from green-dyed goose feathers fixed to wire branches, in turn fixed to a central wooden pole.

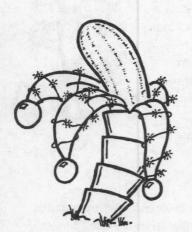

Banana Christmas Tree

With the Indian climate too hot for the traditional fir tree, Indians instead decorate the leaves of a banana or mango tree.

Oil Palm Christmas Tree

With a lack of fir trees in the West African Republic of Liberia, the Liberians instead decorate oil palm trees.

Toilet Brush Tree

With early artificial Christmas trees mostly made of feathers, in the 1930s the Addis Brush Company used their surplus stock of toilet brushes to create the first artificial Christmas brush tree.

Less flammable and capable of carrying the weight of more ornaments than the feather tree, the toilet brush tree proved popular in both the United States and Britain, and the company went into full production using the machinery previously used to manufacture their toilet brushes.

Pre-dating the use of plastic, the brushes were at the time made from tough animal-hair bristles – most commonly plucked from a horse, squirrel or badger.

Aluminium Christmas Tree

Popular in the United States between the late 1950s and early 1960s, the aluminium Christmas tree was, as you might guess, made of aluminium. With fears that draping normal Christmas fairy lights through the tree's aluminium branches would cause a short circuit, the trees were lit from below by a rotating colour wheel divided into wedge-shaped segments of variously coloured plastic.

Whilst some saw aluminium Christmas trees as futuristic, icons of the approaching age of space travel, others regarded them as a symbol of bad taste.

ONE SMALL TREE FOR MAN...

Following the first airing on TV in 1965 of *A Charlie Brown Christmas* (see page 46–47), where Charlie Brown shunned what he saw as the fake over-commercialism of Christmas, the aluminium Christmas tree fell from favour and, by the time man first set foot on the moon, the prime yuletide use for aluminium had turned to wrapping the Christmas turkey.

Pohutukawa

Named by, and held in great honour by the Maori people, who used the tree's leaves and bark as a form of medicine to relieve, amongst other things, dysentery, with bright red flowers that bloom in late December, the pohutukawa is known as the New Zealand Christmas Tree.

Pohutukawa forests once covered great coastal areas of the

54

north of New Zealand's North Island. Despite its famed ability to survive clinging to the edge of the steepest of cliffs, the tree's survival is now under threat from clearing for farming and the introduction of the common brushtail possum, which has a habit of stripping the tree of its foliage.

General Grant Tree

Thought to be around 1,650 years old, the General Grant Tree in Kings Canyon National Park, California, is the United States' official national Christmas tree. Standing 82 metres tall, nearly 36 metres in circumference at the base, and with the trunk estimated to contain 1,320 cubic metres of wood, the giant sequoia is the second largest tree in the world. Discovered in 1862, five years later the tree was named after Ulysses S. Grant, Union Army general and future 18th President of the United States.

Respected as a living memorial to American forces personnel who have lost their lives in service to their country, each year since 1925 park rangers have laid a large wreath at the base of the General Grant Tree.

London's Trafalgar Square Christmas Tree
Twenty metres tall and decorated with 500 white lights, the
Christmas tree in London's Trafalgar Square is a gift each
year from the City of Oslo. Seen as a symbol of peace, the
tree is given as a 'thank you' for the support Britain gave to
occupied Norway during the Second World War.

Section 3

BEARING GIFTS, WE TRAVERSE AFAR

Chapter 9

A TIME FOR GIVING

AT 46 metres in height and weighing 204 metric tonnes, the world's largest gift was the Statue of Liberty, given in 1886 by the people of France to the people of the United States in celebration of their independence.

Christmas is a time for giving, and, on a smaller scale, here are a few suggestions:

Flashing Merry Christmas Comb

Observe the man in your life's eyes light up when he unwraps the Flashing Merry Christmas Comb. He'll be in hysterics. Even funnier if he has no hair!

Chocolate Calculator

The ideal present for your accountant; sit back and laugh picturing him or her attempting to work out your end-of-year accounts before the chocolate melts!

Gentleman's Ball Scratcher

Add a little light relief to a friend's daily commute.

Loo Laughs

Swap the normal sounds of the toilet for laughter with this Loo Laughs toilet roll, packed with jokes, cartoons and hysterical one-liners. Peer through the keyhole and watch as Grandma laughs so much she loses her false teeth down the toilet!

USB Desk Vacuum Cleaner

Surprise your secretary with a USB Miniature Desk Vacuum Cleaner. Sit back and watch as he or she sucks up all the crumbs from their lunchtime sandwich.

Teasub

The ideal gift for a tea-drinking Beatles fan: a miniature yellow plastic submarine with a difference! Watch as they open the Teasub's hatch, fill it with tea leaves and dunk in hot water. Before they can sing, 'We all live in a...', hey presto – the perfect cup of tea!

Sterling Silver Mussel Eater

Is your man a man of muscles? Why not treat him to a Sterling Silver Mussel Eater, moulded from the shell of a real mussel. Unlike your relationship, guaranteed never to lose its shine.

Inflatable Chef's Costume

The perfect present for the friend who loves fancy dress parties but is too embarrassed to travel there dressed in full costume. Arrive at the party; step into the costume; flick the switch on the battery pack and HEY PRESTO!

Divorce Vouchers

After the stresses of Christmas, January is the most popular month for filing for divorce. So, if your relationship is about as exciting as watching paint dry, for less than the price of a decent flat-screen TV, what better present to give your partner in marriage than Divorce Vouchers! Alternatively, a 'must have' gift if your partner is married to someone else!

Chapter 10

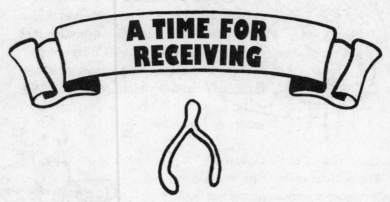

A TIME FOR RECEIVING

Be careful what you wish for...

Camouflage Golf Balls

For the keen golfer who enjoys a large handicap.
  Balls indeed.

Hand-Knitted Reindeer Jumper

As sported by Mark Darcy in *Bridget Jones's Diary*. Lovingly knitted by an elderly relative; guaranteed to never wear out, as you can only ever wear it at Christmas without looking a complete plonker and even then, best worn inside the house only.

Often seen in the pub on Boxing Day; rarely witnessed at other times.

Belly Button Brush

No more worry of unwanted belly-button fluff with this silver-plated belly-button brush.

Just leave it in the presentation box and you can give it away next year.

Musical Piano Tie

Too busy to learn to play the piano? Simply clip the musical piano tie around your shirt collar and press any of the printed keys to produce one of eight musical notes. Can be played anywhere!

Novelty Christmas Underwear

Adorned with the likes of 'I've got BIG Baubles!', novelty Christmas underwear is best kept out of sight at all times.

Unlike the novelty socks, tie or jumper, at least with underwear, when worn, they're normally hidden from view; hence the name: underwear. You can, therefore, happily wear your novelty underwear all year round.

Snow Globe

If there's no snow at Christmas, don't be miserable. Just because you can't make a snowman, have a snowball fight or go sledging, there's always hours of fun to be had with a plastic snow globe.

Clockwork Meerkats

Not just one but a pair of bow tie and fez-wearing clockwork meerkats to race against one another. Wind them up and watch as they weave about, collide… and disappear straight into the bin.

Battery-operated Talking Polly Parrot

Polly repeats what you say, parrot-fashion! Speak a few words to this plastic parrot and she will immediately repeat them back to you, obscenities and all!

Teach Polly to say something silly then take to the charity shop.

Leopard Print Mankini

What not to wear this summer.

Slippers

One of the most dangerous of Christmas presents, according to a government report, more accidents in the home are caused by carpet slippers than by any other type of clothing. They're not called slippers for nothing.

Section 4

NOT A CREATURE WAS STIRRING

Chapter 11

BARKING MAD!

ACCORDING to commonly quoted figures, around 70 per cent of dogs in Great Britain receive a Christmas present from their owners.

Time to wag the tail of some yuletide creatures...

Donkey
The animal that carried the heavily pregnant Mary to Bethlehem before giving birth to the baby Jesus, the donkey has strong ties with Christmas.

Regarded as a bringer of health and good luck, for many centuries from early Christian times, dark hairs removed from a

donkey's hind quarters were worn in lucky charms, with a belief that the hairs would bring relief from such ailments as toothache and fits.

Before the medical advancements of vaccination and antibiotics, a child suffering from whooping cough would be passed three times between the legs and over the back of a donkey.

Originating from a desert environment, where food is scarce, almost all of what a donkey eats is broken down, and every last bit of goodness extracted. Consequently, donkey manure does not make for a good fertiliser.

And, coming from the desert, their fur is not waterproof.

In southern Spain the giant 'Andalucian-Cordobesan' donkey can grow as large as a racehorse.

Popularly regarded as not the sharpest tool in the box, donkeys are, in reality, highly intelligent…

...and, when matched for weight, stronger than horses.

Being present at the birth of the baby Jesus, no Christmas nativity play would be complete without the humble donkey.

Robin

The UK's national bird, red-breasted robins are a traditional symbol of Christmas. One of the few birds to be heard in the garden on a cold December morning, male red-breasted robins are highly territorial, singing to ward off other males that stray into their territory.

Not a bird to avoid confrontation, it's estimated that up to one in 10 adult male robin deaths are at the beaks of another male.

In Victorian times, postmen in England were commonly referred to as 'robins'. With the Post Office set up to carry royal mail and the colour red being associated with royalty, postmen's uniforms, top hat included, were originally red, the colour of the robin's breast.

Turtle Dove
Nothing to do with amphibious reptiles, the turtle dove gained its name from its 'turr turr' calling sound.

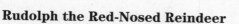

Rudolph the Red-Nosed Reindeer

Every Christmas, as a goodwill gesture, Chicago-based department store, Montgomery Ward, would buy colouring books to give away to visiting children.

In a move to save money by creating their own book, in 1939, Montgomery Ward asked one of their staff advertising copywriters, Robert L. May, to come up with a cheerful animal story. May's four-year-old daughter loved the deer in Chicago Zoo, and so, having decided the star of his Christmas story would be a reindeer, May then needed a name. Rejecting Rollo and Reginald, 'Rudolph the Red-Nosed Reindeer' was born.

Written as an illustrated poem, in the first year of publication, 2.4 million copies of Rudolph's story were given away. With restrictions on the use of paper during the Second World War, the booklet wasn't reissued until 1946, when

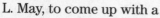

another 3.6 million copies were again given away.

Popularly thought of as Santa's ninth reindeer, lighting the way with his bright nose, Rudolph the Red-Nosed Reindeer has become one of the most endearing and beloved of Christmas characters.

Chapter 12

WHEN A CHILD IS BORN

WHEN *Treasure Island* author Robert Louis Stevenson died, he stipulated in his will that his 13 November birthday should be bequeathed to a friend who disliked being born close to Christmas.

Every year, around half a million babies are born on Christmas Day. Here are some of the more notable…

Isaac Newton

Sir Isaac Newton, revered as one of the world's greatest scientists, was born on Christmas Day, 1642.

It is said that whilst seated under a tree, a falling apple inspired Newton to formulate his theory as to the existence of a gravitational force.

A descendant of the apple tree can be found outside the main gate of Trinity College, Cambridge, close to the room where Newton lived during his studies.

Shane MacGowan

As co-writer of 'Fairytale of New York', frequently voted the UK's most popular Christmas song, it could be considered rather fitting that The Pogues' lead singer and songwriter, Shane MacGowan, was born on Christmas Day, 1957.

Quentin Crisp

Writer, raconteur, and 1970s icon of homosexuality, Quentin Crisp, was born on Christmas Day, 1908.

After his application to enlist in the British Army at the start of the Second World War was rejected by the medical board on the premise he was 'suffering from sexual perversion', in 1942 Crisp began working as a life-drawing class model. Describing the work as being 'like a civil servant, except that you were naked', in 1968 Crisp published his memoirs, *The Naked Civil Servant*, recounting life in a homophobic British society. Its adaption into a TV film in 1975 turned him into a star.

Kenny Everett

Renowned for his wacky UK radio and TV shows, Kenny Everett was born on Christmas Day, 1944.

Beginning his career as a DJ on pirate radio, over the next 20 years Everett rebounded from one radio station to another, after repeatedly getting the sack for his outspoken comments.

Moving to television, the *Kenny Everett Video Show* and later *Television Show* featured such characters as Mr Angry of Mayfair, a City gent who would, after complaining of the programme's content, turn away from camera to reveal women's underwear in lieu of the entire back half of his suit.

Lew Grade

The TV producer and media boss responsible for bringing such programmes as *The Muppet Show*, *The Saint*, *Danger Man* and *The Prisoner* to the small screen, Lew Grade, was born on Christmas Day, 1906.

In 1980, Grade's own television production company, ITC Entertainment, financed the star-studded film, *Raise the Titanic*. Sinking badly at the box office, at the time Grade remarked that, in making the film, it would have cost the company less to lower the Atlantic!

Humphrey Bogart

Star of such classic films as *The Maltese Falcon*, *The African Queen* and *Casablanca*, Humphrey Bogart was born on Christmas Day, 1899.

Honoured by the American Film Institute as the country's greatest male screen legend, Bogart is credited with six of the Institute's 100 Greatest Movie Quotes of all time.

But he never did say, 'Play it again, Sam'.

Chapter 13

O LITTLE TOWN OF BETHLEHEM

...and a few other Christmas-sounding places.

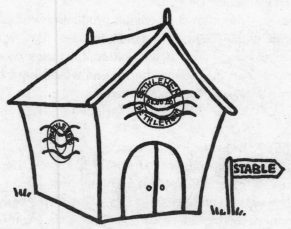

Bethlehem

On the very northwestern edge of the Brecon Beacons National Park in Wales is the tiny farming village of Bethlehem. Named after the local Nonconformist chapel, if you can't get to the Middle East, then this is the place to visit if you wish to give your Christmas cards a Bethlehem postmark.

You know it makes franking-sense.

Christmas Common

In the heart of the Chiltern Hills in Oxfordshire sits Christmas Common. On the route of the 68-mile Oxfordshire Way footpath between Bourton-on-the-Water and Henley-on-Thames, the tiny hamlet is a good starting point for walks and cycling, followed by a spot of light refreshment at the Fox and Hounds pub.

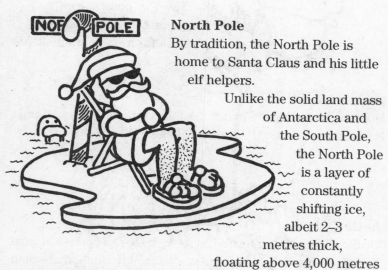

North Pole

By tradition, the North Pole is home to Santa Claus and his little elf helpers.

Unlike the solid land mass of Antarctica and the South Pole, the North Pole is a layer of constantly shifting ice, albeit 2–3 metres thick, floating above 4,000 metres of very cold Arctic Ocean water. It's predicted that, due to the effects of climate change, the North Pole will almost certainly become ice-free at times during future years.

Christmas Pie

The hamlet of Christmas Pie, part of the Parish of Normandy near the Surrey town of Guildford, is named after Christmas Pie Farm, owned in the early seventeenth century by a local family with the surname 'Christmas'.

The 'Pie' comes from 'pightel', the Anglo-Saxon term for a small arable field.

Turkey Island

Don't be fooled by the name. Six miles inland, Turkey Island is a hamlet near the Hampshire village of Shedfield.

Snow Falls

Setting off from the village of Ingleton, the five-mile circular Ingleton Waterfalls Trail passes some of the most impressive waterfalls in North Yorkshire, including Hollybush Spout and Snow Falls.

Christmas Island

Kiritimati, otherwise known as Christmas Island, may sound like the ideal location for a get-away-from-it-all romantic winter break, were it not for the fact that between 1956 and 1958 Britain used the raised coral atoll in the northern Pacific Ocean to conduct nuclear tests of the hydrogen bomb.

Chapter 14

OH! WHAT FUN IT IS TO RIDE

SPEAKING of travel…

Under the Freedom of Information Act, in December 2011 Cheltenham Borough Council was asked to provide details of its contingency plans were Santa Claus to crash his sleigh whilst delivering presents on Christmas Eve.

From Santa's Sleigh to a Christmas Bullet, time to hop on board some Yuletide transport…

Santa's Sleigh

Scientific boffins have calculated that, in order to deliver presents to all of the world's well-behaved children as they sleep on Christmas Eve, Santa has to visit 91.8 million homes.

Travelling east to west to benefit from Earth's different time zones, and allowing for the reindeer to have one or two refreshment breaks, over a maximum 31-hour working shift, this comes out at 822.6 home visits per second. Covering a distance of around 75 million miles, Santa needs to travel at an average speed of 671 miles per second, or 2,415,600 miles per hour; 3,145 times the speed of sound.

Roller skates

Each day between 16 and 24 December in Caracas, the capital of Venezuela, Catholic churchgoers attend an early morning mass. With streets shut off to traffic, the churchgoers arrive on roller skates. The night before, as they climb into bed, children knot the end of a length of string to their big toe, dangling the other end out of the bedroom window.

The next morning, as they pass by, the roller-skating churchgoers give a tug to the dangling strings.

Sledge

A sledge is a very useful form of transport when travelling downhill in snow. If improvising with a plastic tray, first remove all teacups and other crockery. Remember to wear knee and elbow guards, shin pads, shoulder guards and, most importantly, a helmet. The good old days of reckless fun are long gone in the modern health-and-safety-conscious world.

Much modern-day sledging fun is to be had attempting to bowl over television camera crews reporting on the health-and-safety dangers of sledging.

Christmas Bullet

With no aeronautical or aircraft design experience, in 1910 medical doctor William Christmas founded the Christmas Aeroplane Company. Based in Washington, D.C., Christmas set about designing the Christmas Bullet, an all-wood single-seat cantilever biplane.

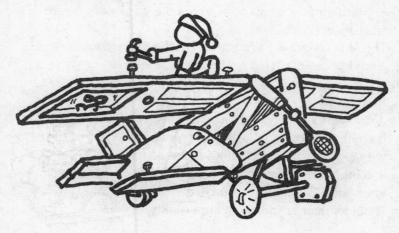

Using scrounged wood and other materials not suitable for aircraft construction, the Christmas Bullet is considered to be amongst the worst aircraft ever constructed.

Lacking any struts or braces, on its maiden flight in January 1919, the Christmas Bullet's wings fell off, the plane destroyed beyond repair.

Undeterred, Christmas built a second prototype, again destroyed on its maiden flight.

Neither of the pilots lived to tell the tale, and no more Christmas Bullets were built.

I SAW THREE SHIPS WASSAILING IN

Chapter 15

GOOD TIDINGS WE BRING

SEEN today in the Christmas tradition of carol singers on the doorstep, wassailing dates back to medieval times, the word 'wassail' coming from the Anglo-Saxon toast, 'Be thou hale', a call for good health. Peasant workers of the land would visit the landowner and exchange their blessing and goodwill for food and drink. The blessing would take the form of a song: a carol such as 'We Wish You a Merry Christmas'.

Apple Wassail

> *Wassaile the trees, that they may beare,*
> *You many a plum and many a pear;*
> *For more or lesse fruits they will bring,*
> *As you do give them Wassailing.*

The apple wassail is the annual custom of singing to trees in apple orchards in Devon, Somerset and other cider-producing counties of south-west England in order to scare away evil spirits and encourage a good harvest for the following autumn.

Adorned with a crown made of freshly gathered ivy, lichen and mistletoe, the Wassail Queen, accompanied by her Princess, leads a procession to the nearest orchard, whereby the Queen is lifted into the branches of the biggest apple tree.

Whilst the villagers form a circle around the tree and pour hot mulled wassail cider on its roots, the Princess passes the Queen some cider-soaked toast, which she dutifully ties amongst the branches as a gift to the tree spirits.

The Queen then recites the following verse:

> *Here's to thee, old apple tree*
> *That blooms well, bears well.*
> *Hats full, caps full,*
> *An' all under one tree.*
> *Hurrah! Hurrah!*

...After which the assembled crowd sings, shouts, bangs drums and pots and pans, and generally makes as much noise as possible...

89

…until several farmers fire their rifles through the branches of the tree.

If still alive, the Wassail Queen is then lowered down, and the semi-drunken rabble move on to the next orchard.

Originating as an Anglo-Saxon pagan ritual, the wassail should be celebrated on the evening of 5 January, the Twelfth Night, although it is more popularly celebrated 12 days later on 17 January, 'Old Twelvy Night' – what would have been the correct date before the introduction of the Gregorian calendar in 1752.

Still very much thriving today, the apple wassail can be found, amongst other places, at both Carhampton in Somerset and Whimple in Devon.

Wassail Punch

> *Wassail! Wassail! All over town,*
> *Our toast it is white and our ale it is brown;*
> *Our bowl it is made of the white maple tree;*
> *With the wassailing bowl, we'll drink to thee.*

A hot mulled cider punch often drunk at Christmas time, and more traditionally as an integral part of the wassail

ceremony, wassail punch can be made with ginger, cinnamon, sugar, and nutmeg, with fruit juice, wine, sherry, brandy, mulled beer or even mead, as long as it is topped with slices of toast.

Lamb's Wool

Far from being something found on a lamb, Lamb's Wool is a variety of wassail punch made from traditional ale, sugar and baked apples, spiced with nutmeg, ginger and cinnamon.

Wassail Puzzle Jug

Strangely, not so popular in pubs nowadays, a wassail puzzle jug was a large jug with a spout that had a number of small holes hidden in the neck. As an unsuspecting drinker attempted to down the jug's contents, he or she would be soaked from the wassail punch pouring from the holes.

It's funny what passed for entertainment before pool tables and gaming machines.

Chapter 16

MUM'S THE WORD

KNOWN as 'gusards' in Scotland, 'murmuring' in Canada, 'mumping' in Warwickshire and 'corning' in Kent, 'mumming' – from the old German word for a disguised person – was originally little more than a thinly veiled pagan excuse for Christmas entertainment. Men and women would swap clothes, adorn masks and call upon their unsuspecting neighbours, where – welcomed or not – they would sing, dance and perform a simple, comical play.

The mummers play would generally feature a conflict between good and evil, the English traditional hero of King, or Saint George, slaying or being slain by either the evil Turkish Knight, or a noble soldier by the dubious name of Slasher.

In would then step the Quack Doctor, to resurrect the dead character, courtesy of his or her magic potion.

Along the way, the mummers' leader and narrator of the play, dressed as Father Christmas, would introduce such characters as Crumpin John, Indian Dart, Beelzebub (sometimes known as Eezum Squeezum), Robin Hood and Little Devil Doubt.

By medieval times, mumming had slid down the slippery slope towards out-and-out begging, until, in the sixteenth century, King Henry VIII passed a law declaring that anyone caught mumming wearing a mask would be thrown into gaol for three months.

King Henry VIII may be long gone, but mumming is still alive and well in Britain today. It rears its head at Christmas time in the form of plays performed either door to door, in the streets or in pubs, perpetrators of the so-called 'entertainment' evading lengthy gaol sentences by painting their faces black or red and masquerading under the guise of local names such as galoshins, tipteerers, soulers, rhymers and guisers.

If you see one, I suggest you call the local police.

Belsnicklers

A form of mumming, as part of Christmas celebrations in the Canadian province of Nova Scotia, masked 'belsnicklers' pass through towns and villages, banging on doors, ringing bells and making a general nuisance of themselves. When identified, the belsnicklers remove their costumes and give out sweets to children who claim to have been good.

'Owd 'Oss

> *Jim Slack 'e 'ad a grey 'oss,*
> *Such an 'oss as you nev-er did see;*
> *Wi' a lump on 'is rump an' 'is owd tail,*
> *An 'is legs bent aht an' blind in one e'e.*

Not unlike a Mumming play, an 'Owd 'Oss play was once popularly performed in streets and pubs around Christmas time in parts of Britain.

An 'old horse' took the lead role, originally a real horse's skull, painted black and red, would be mounted on a pole, then held aloft by an 'actor' hidden under a small cloth, pretending to be the horse's body.

Whilst the 'actor' operated the horse's snapping jaw, the accompanying group of men would sing their rendition of 'The Old Horse', a song about a horse fit for little more than the knackers' yard.

95

Popular between the late nineteenth and early twentieth centuries, the knackered old horse still rears its head in parts of Britain today, particularly in the counties of Yorkshire, Derbyshire and Nottinghamshire. Although, with modern laws regarding the disposal of animal remains no longer including severing a horse's head, painting it black and red, sticking it on a pole and operating its jaw with a stick, the modern 'Old 'Oss tends to be less animal skull and more cow gum and papier-mâché.

Derby Tup

Here comes me an' ahr owd lass,
Short o'money an' short o' brass.
Pay for a pint and let us sup,
Then we'll show yer the Derby Tup.

Similar to a mumming or 'Owd 'Oss play, the Derby Tup is a traditional English play celebrating the 'Derby Ram' folksong, once popularly performed by groups of boys around Christmas time, in and around Derbyshire.

'Tup' being an old word for 'ram', the Derby Tup replaced the horse's head of the 'Owd 'Oss play with that of a sheep. The 'Tup' was more often than not a broomstick with a rough wooden sheep's head attached, held aloft by a boy covered in a sack.

A rather short play, the plot would generally involve The Tup being killed by The Butcher, whilst the remaining boys – often with faces painted black or red – recounted the verses of the 'Derby Ram'.

The Derby Tup still meets its end under the butcher's knife to this present day, kept alive by the Cambridge-based, Northstow Mummers, with the added mummers' bonus of the sheep being resurrected by a quack doctor.

Mari Lwyd

A cross between wassailing and mumming, Mari Lwyd involves a horse's head with a snapping jaw, uninvited door-to-door visits, alcohol and general merriment.

The difference is: it's in Wales.

Similar to the four-legged star of an 'Owd 'Oss play, the 'horse' is provided by either a horse's skull, or a piece of wood rigged with a spring-loaded jaw, bandaged to look like a genuine horse's head. Held aloft by an 'actor', both actor and horse are draped in a white sheet. Cloth ears are sewn onto the sheet, coloured ribbons fixed to the skull, bells attached to the reins, and eye-sockets provided by green bottle-ends.

Dating back to pagan times, the ancient tradition involves the arrival of the Mari Lwyd and its party at the door of a pub or house, where, in the hope of gaining entry, the gathered party sing and exchange rhyming insults with the occupants.

Once inside, as the party sing another traditional song, the 'horse' runs around, snapping its jaws, all the while the leader of the group 'attempting' to restrain it. Anyone 'bit' is subject to paying a 'fine', usually the providing of food or a glass of ale.

Translating as 'Grey Mare', Mari Lwyd was once widely practised throughout Wales, in particular in the southern counties of Glamorgan and Gwent, to mark the passing of the winter solstice. It's still practised around Christmas time in such places as Cowbridge and Llantrisant, and, every New Year's Day, in the village of Llangynwyd.

Chapter 17

CUSTOM-A-RELATIONS

IN FINLAND, a sauna is seen as a symbol of purity, a holy place where women give birth and the sick are healed.

On Christmas Eve, before celebrations begin, it is the tradition for the people of Finland to visit a sauna.

Time to open the door and peer through the steam at a few of the Yuletide customs and traditions observed around the world...

Scroggling the Holly

Christmas begins in the English village of Haworth with a ceremony known as Scroggling the Holly. Held mid-November, the start of the festive season is marked by a parade of costumed pixies and fairies

sprinkling fairy dust along the cobbled Main Street, whilst the Ivy Princess and attendant entourage hand out sprigs of holly to onlookers.

The following day, prancing Morris dancers gaily lead a procession of children in traditional Victorian dress, who follow the Holly Queen up the cobbled street to the steps of St Michael and All Angels Parish church.

A crowning ceremony is duly held for the Queen, who then proceeds to unlock the church gates and welcome the spirit of Christmas into the West Yorkshire village.

Once welcomed, Santa Claus arrives with his wife, Mrs Claus, to spread Christmas cheer.

Ashen Faggot

It may sound like a burnt meatball destined for the food waste bin, but the Ashen Faggot is a very old English custom, still practised on the West Country moors of Dartmoor.

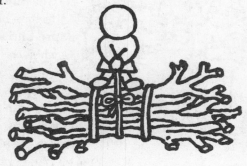

A bundle of sticks, twigs or branches from an ash tree are bound with nine flexible ash strips known as 'withies'. On Christmas Eve, with a fire lit using the remains of the previous year's faggots, the new 'ashen faggots' are thrown to the flames. As the fire takes hold and each withy splits, the onlookers celebrate with a drink – most commonly cider.

According to tradition, unmarried women each pick a faggot, with a belief that the first one whose withy splits will be the next to marry.

The custom is thought to have come from Scandinavia, where, in Norse mythology, the ash tree was held sacred as the 'tree of life'. The tree would be burned at their Christmas feast in honour of their god, Thor.

101

Yule Goat

Speaking of Thor, the origins of the Scandinavian Yule Goat are thought to date back to pre-Christian times, when the Norse god, wielding a special hammer said to be capable of flattening a mountain, would fly through the sky in a chariot pulled by two goats.

One day, laying on a special meal for his hungry guests, Thor kills and cooks the goats. The following day, realising that without his goats his chariot will no longer fly, he uses his special hammer to bring them back to life.

Originally thought invisible and watching over Christmas preparations, during the nineteenth century the Yule Goat began to take on the role of Santa Claus, becoming the giver of Christmas gifts, with one of the male members of the family dressing up accordingly.

Today in Finland and Scandinavia, the Yule Goat mostly makes its appearance either in the form of a small Christmas decoration made of straw tied by a red ribbon, or as a giant version on display in town and city centres. Unfortunately, being made of straw, most Yule Goats tend not to make it through to Christmas, becoming victims of arson attacks.

The most famous of these straw Yule Goats is the Gävle Goat, displayed each year in the Swedish town of Gävle. First erected in 1966, the 13-metre tall goat lasted until the stroke of midnight on New Year's Eve before being set alight. Since then the Gävle Goat has boasted a less than 50 per cent survival rate.

To add insult to arson attack, one year the goat met its end under the wheels of a car.

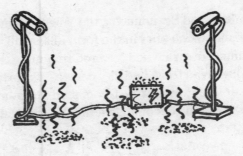

In 1996, webcams were introduced to keep a safe eye on the straw goat. Alas, with little success.

Security guards were posted, still to no avail.

In 2005 the Gävle Goat lasted barely a week, razed to the ground in early December. The gloves were finally off, and the following year the giant straw goat was treated with a fireproofing substance normally used on the interior of aeroplanes. Cutting down on the now-unnecessary guard protection, the Goat Committee boldly claimed that the goat would never burn again, resistant to even a napalm attack.

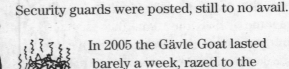

Aside from a scorched leg (and putting a damper on a humorous end to the story), the goat survived.

Juleoffer

In remembrance of Thor's Yule Goats, up until the mid-twentieth century, particularly in Sweden, the custom of Juleoffer was practised each year at Christmas time.

The Juleoffer, or Christmas sacrifice, suitably goat-attired and with a large pair of horns, would be shepherded into a crowded room by two men. Whilst singing verses of a song referring to cloaks of various colours, the men would then pretend to slaughter the poor unfortunate, all the while covering him with correspondingly coloured cloaks.

As the song ends, the Yule Goat, having pretended to be dead, would jump up and skip about, much to the delight of the watching crowd.

Caganer

Where Scandinavian homes have Yule Goat ornaments made of straw, homes in Catalonia and neighbouring areas of Spain, Portugal and southern Italy have a Caganer.

Traditionally represented as a Catalan peasant man with a red barretina hat, the small figurine is hidden in nativity scenes of Bethlehem, squatting with his pants around his ankles in the act of defecation.

With the origin of placing a defecating figurine in a nativity scene lost to posterity, of the many possible reasons put forward, the most plausible is that the Caganer, by creating faeces, is bringing nutrients to the earth, enriching the soil and therefore ensuring a good harvest over the coming year.

The Caganer is also said to embody human equality, in that, regardless of sex, race or social standing, everyone defecates.

In 2005, the Spanish city of Barcelona publically displayed a nativity scene which failed to include a Caganer. With Barcelona the capital of Catalonia, many viewed this as disrespectful of local traditions. The city council attempted to defend its position by countering that the Caganer was not included because a recently introduced by-law had made both urination and defecation in public illegal.

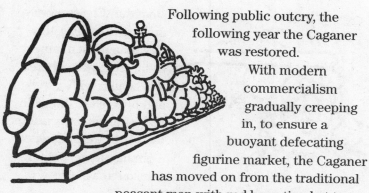

Following public outcry, the following year the Caganer was restored.

With modern commercialism gradually creeping in, to ensure a buoyant defecating figurine market, the Caganer has moved on from the traditional peasant man with red barretina hat to everything from squatting nuns, celebrities and Santa Claus to Spanish and British royalty.

Tió de Nadal

References to defecation are common in Catalan folklore, a popular pre-meal toast politely translating as 'eat well, defecate a good deal and don't be afraid of death!'

Not dissimilar to the traditional Yule log, the Tió de Nadal, the Log of Christmas, is a hollowed-out wooden log given pride of place on the yuletide Catalan dining table. Propped up on four stick legs, the Cago Tió, as it is popularly known, is painted with a grinning face and given a little red barretina hat.

Every night from 8 December, the day of the Feast of the Immaculate Conception, the Cago Tió is 'fed' sweets and nuts and then wrapped in a blanket to protect against the night-time cold.

On either Christmas Eve or Christmas Day, the Cago Tió is then moved to the fireplace, where it is beaten with a stick and ordered to defecate. Encouragement is offered by way of the singing of a popular song, politely translated as:

Poo log,
Log of Christmas;
Don't poo herrings
Which are too salty,
Poo turrón,
Which is much better!

Once the log has excreted its *turrón* – a type of nougat popular in Spain at Christmas – the Caga Tió is given one last push to reveal either an onion, head of garlic or a salted herring.

Drawing Straws

In Belarus and other Eastern European countries before the traditional Christmas Eve supper, straw is spread on the table in remembrance of the stable where Jesus was born. In turn, guests remove straw from the table to foresee their future, and it is from this tradition that we get the practice of 'drawing straws' as a way of decision-making.

Meanwhile, unmarried Belarusian women predict their future relationship status by playing a game that involves a chicken. The women form a circle, each clasping a handful of corn. Whoever's hand the chicken first eats corn from it is thought will be the next to marry.

Goose Bumps

Similar to Belarus, in Germany it is traditional for a group of single women to form a circle, having first blindfolded a goose. The first woman the goose bumps into it's believed will be the next to wed.

Wool Tossing

In Britain, if an unmarried woman tosses a ball of wool to the sky on Christmas Eve, it is said that, when the wool lands, it will unravel to reveal the face of her future husband.

Feeding the Wren

Legend tells St Stephen, the first Christian martyr, was hiding in a holly bush, when a wren bird landed on the bush and sang a little song, betraying him to his Roman pursuers.

To this day in parts of Ireland on 26 December, St Stephen's Day, children follow the custom of Feeding the Wren. With an effigy of a wren bird fixed to a holly bush on a long pole, the youngsters travel from door to door collecting money for the poor.

The Norwegian Bird Dance

An early Christmas tradition amongst Norwegian farmers begins at the late autumn harvest. Before harvesting, a farmer will gather a sheath of wheat and tie it to a tree branch. A circle of snow beneath the branch is then cleared, giving the birds their own little dance floor, where they can happily waltz, samba  or tango the afternoon away, until ready for their next meal.

Just before sunset, the farmer checks on the wheat. If the birds are enjoying a hearty feast, it is thought to be a sign that the harvest will be good.

The Maya Deer Dance

In the Central American country of Belize, from the evening of 22 December the local people of the Maya village of Santa Cruz begin a five-night celebration of the 'Deer Dance'. The festival, a reminder of the bond between nature and humankind, involves 24 colourfully costumed performers. With the costumes

111

including several dogs, a jaguar, a joker, a man dressed as an older woman, and a number of 'sacred deer', amid ritualised dancing, whilst the deer are hunted by the dogs, the jaguar 'kidnaps' a man dressed as a maiden. In turn, the jaguar is pursued by a hunter; all the while the joker looks on, poking fun at performers and onlookers.

It's funny what passes for entertainment…

Nut Cracking
In Slovakia, at the end of the Christmas Eve supper, it is customary for each member of the family to crack open a walnut. Each quarter of the walnut is believed to represent a quarter of the year, and for each section that is healthy, it's believed the person will have a healthy three months.

However, for each section of the walnut that is rotten, that quarter of the coming year will in turn be rotten.

A candle is then blown out by the eldest person at the table. If the smoke rises, they will have good luck. Should the smoke sink, they will have, at best, bad luck; at worst, death may not be far away.

Once the eldest person has discovered his or her fate, the candle is relit and given to the next eldest at the table, until all have taken their turn.

Ox-tails

As part of Christmas celebrations, in the US city of New Orleans, a large ox decorated with ribbons and holly is paraded through the streets.

I wouldn't imagine the ox is best pleased!

The Night of the Radishes

Sounding like a low-budget remake of *The Day of the Triffids*, The Night of the Radishes is a spectacular Christmas festival, held each 23 December in the Mexican city of Oaxaca.

With roots traceable back to 1897, each year thousands of onlookers gather to admire giant, specially grown radishes, intricately carved to depict anything from animals and dancers to kings and saints.

Els Enfarinats

Commemorating the biblical tale of the murder of all male children in Bethlehem by King Herod, on 28 December, Holy Innocents' Day, boys in Spanish villages and towns light bonfires. Meanwhile one boy, duly elected Mayor, orders adults to perform duties such as street-sweeping and refuse collection.

Taking the 200-year-old tradition somewhat further, in the town of Ibi, the day begins at sunrise with a group of 14 young men, faces hidden by flour and dressed in military uniform, staging a mock coup d'état. Having 'captured' the town, members of the Els Enfarinats are duly elected to positions of public office.

Opposing forces wearing top hats decorated with paper stars gather, confronting the new town governors with the intention of removing them from office.

As fighting ensues, 'fines' are requested from local businesses and onlookers, a refusal to pay resulting in a liberal covering of flour.

The afternoon ends with a full-scale battle waged in the town square, with the throwing of flour bombs, eggs, and a liberal misuse of jumping-jack firecrackers.

Chapter 18

MYTH STORY

FROM an unbelievably smelly malicious goblin with horse's legs and goat's ears to a shape-shifting cyclopean farmer in red and grey knitwear, time to peer through the mist at a few Christmas myths, folktales and legends...

Kallikantzaros

Half-animal, half-human, with horse's legs, goat's ears, monkey's arms and ferocious tusks, a huge head, long tongue, glaring eyes and unbelievably smelly...
A Kallikantzaros is not an ideal Christmas guest.

In Greek legend, the goblin-like creatures emerge from their dank underground dens to play pranks and create mischievous havoc.

To stop a Kallikantzaros getting into your home you must keep a large fire burning to prevent it from sneaking down the chimney. You must also burn an old, smelly shoe.

Outside, you should hang a pig's jawbone by the door, and leave a colander on the doorstep. Creatures of the night, if a Kallikantzaros approaches it will be distracted from its evil doings by sitting and counting the colander's holes until the sun rises and it is forced to return underground. Not that many Kallikantzaroi reach sunrise: since three is a holy number, to count above the number two proves lethal.

Legend tells that any baby born during the Twelve Days of Christmas is at risk, upon reaching adulthood, of turning each Yuletide into a Kallikantzaros. This dreadful fate can be avoided by either strapping the baby in locks of straw or garlic, or singeing the child's toenails.

Personally, I'd plump for the straw.

Badalisc

Resembling a giant slug, with a huge head, horns, gaping mouth and blazing eyes, the Badalisc is a mythical creature that is said to live in the woods around the village of Andrista, in the Italian Alpine valley of Camonica.

Somewhat shy and not being one for making personal appearances, each year, on the eve of Epiphany, it is the task of one of the villagers to dress up as the mythical creature and retreat to the woods, only to be 'captured' by a parade of drum-beating male villagers masquerading as old witches, bearded shepherds and a hunchback.

Once returned to the village, the Badalisc is called upon to make a speech recounting local gossip, but, being a dumb animal with little grasp of the Italian language, the speech, written in rhymes, is made by the creature's 'spokesperson'.

The following day, the Badalisc is free to return to the woods.

It's funny what passes for entertainment in the Italian Alps.

Babushka

There once lived, in a small Russian village, an old woman called Babushka. Always cooking, cleaning and gardening, Babushka was so busy keeping her home and garden tidy, she paid little attention to the new star that had appeared in the sky.

The next day, three kings came knocking at the door, looking for somewhere to stay until setting off again at nightfall to follow the new star, which they believed would lead them to the newborn king.

Later that day, the kings invited Babushka to come with them, but she was too busy keeping her house in order.

Eventually, having tidied her home and caught up on her sleep, she set off to find the three kings, and, after many days, arrived in Bethlehem. By this time the kings had taken the new baby Jesus off to Egypt. Sadly, she was too late. It is said that Babushka is, to this day, still looking for the newborn king, and, on the Eve of Christmas, she visits the families of Russia, leaving gifts in the hope that one of their children may be the baby Jesus.

A heart-warming traditional Russian folktale, and yet most Russians appear to have never heard of the story. The tale of Babushka was most likely created in 1907 by Edith Matilda Thomas, an American writer and poet, having come across the almost identical Italian legend of La Befana. In Italy, La

Befana is often referred to as La Vecchia – 'the old woman or grandmother', which translates into Russian as 'Babushka'.

Thomas's poem, *Babushka: The Russian Legend*, proved so popular that it was retold by several other authors until eventually the origin of the tale was lost and the story has become a 'Russian legend', albeit existing only in America.

La Befana

Speaking of La Befana, each year, on the night of 5 January, the kindly witch is said to soar through the night sky on her broomstick, delivering gifts to sleeping Italian children. Sweets for those who have been good…

…onions, garlic and lumps of black coal for those who have run their parents ragged and almost been put up for adoption.

The Befana comes at night
With her shoes all broken
With a dress in Roman style
Up, up with the Befana.

Snegurochka

Sounding like a cross between a
snorkel and a brand of Russian
vodka, according to Old Slavic and
pagan folklore, Snegurochka – the
Snow Maiden – is a snow sculpture
that comes alive.

Adopted by a childless
peasant couple, Snegurochka
later befriends a young
shepherd. She asks her
mother for a heart so that
she may love him,
but the warmth of
her heart melts her.

A less romantic story tells that Snegurochka melts away
when she is dared to jump over a bonfire on the eve of the
summer solstice.

In Russia, Snegurochka is seen
as the granddaughter of Father
Frost, accompanying him in
his horse-drawn sledge and
helping him deliver presents
to children at Christmas time.

Grýla and Leppalothi

According to thirteenth-
century folklore, there once
lived, in the mountains of
Iceland, two hideous troll-
like ogres: Grýla
and Leppalothi.

Grýla, by all accounts
lacking her husband's
looks, was described in
Jón Árnason's nineteenth-
century collection of
folktales as having three
heads, each head with goat's horns, huge ears and a long
knotted beard. In each of her hands she clutched three eyes.

Further descriptions of Grýla saw her with 15 tails,
each tail holding 100 sacks, each sack full to the brim with
naughty children, stolen from their families at Christmas
time. There was nothing Grýla enjoyed more than to feast
on the flesh of a naughty child!

To this day, the story of Grýla
and Leppalothi is recounted
to children by Icelandic
parents as a warning of
what will happen if they
continue to misbehave.

The Yule Lads

Sheep-Cote Clod, Gully Gawk, Stubby, Spoon Licker, Pot Scraper, Bowl Licker, Window Peeper, Door Slammer, Skyr Gobbler, Sausage Swiper, Door Sniffer, Meat Hook and Candle Beggar: the English translations of the names of the 13 children of Grýla and Leppalothi.

Having inherited their parents' ogre-like qualities, it is said that each day from 12 December, one of the Yule Lads – known in Iceland as Jolasveinar – would descend from the mountains to prey upon farmers' sheep, steal food, peer through windows, slam doors and generally make a nuisance of themselves.

Today the elf and goblin-like Yule Lads are responsible for gift giving, each day leaving a small present in the shoe of a 'good' child, or a potato or similar in the shoe of one deemed 'bad'.

On Christmas Day the Yule Lads start to return to the mountains, the last one returning on 6 January, the final day of Christmas.

Yule Cat

Bigger than a lion and not nearly as cuddly, the Yule Cat is the pet of the Yule Lads and their ogre parents, Grýla and Leppalothi.

It is said that the giant black cat has a taste for devouring children who have either been too lazy to have earned the money to buy, or be rewarded by, the gift of a new item of clothing before Christmas.

St Barbara

One of the Fourteen Holy Helper Saints, according to legend, St Barbara – the patron saint of miners, gunsmiths, artillerymen, military engineers and others who work with explosives…

…not to mention firemen, mathematicians, fever and sudden death…

…was the daughter of the pagan emperor, Dioscorus of Asia Minor – what is today, Turkey.

The story tells, wishing his daughter to remain a virgin, whenever Dioscorus was away he kept Barbara locked up in a tower.

The tower had only two windows, but one day Dioscorus returned to find that there were three.

Suspicious that his daughter's virginity might have been compromised by someone in the building trade, the father forced Barbara to confess that, whilst he was away, she had converted to Christianity, and the three windows symbolised the Holy Trinity of her newfound faith.

Dioscorus demanded his daughter brick up the new window and give up this sacrilegious behaviour, but Barbara refused, and so Dioscorus was left with little choice but to have her tortured and beheaded.

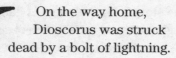

On the way home, Dioscorus was struck dead by a bolt of lightning.

Legend further tells that during Barbara's enforced and lonely imprisonment in the tower, she came across a dried-up cherry tree branch.

She put the branch in a pot and gave it a few drops of water each day until, on Christmas Eve, beautiful cherry blossoms appeared.

To this day, in Catholic parts of Europe on 4 December, the Feast Day of St Barbara, it is customary for a girl to remove a small branch from a cherry tree and place it in water in a warm room.

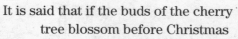

It is said that if the buds of the cherry tree blossom before Christmas Eve then she will marry the following year.

With its roots in pre-Christian pagan times and no reference to the legendary tale of St Barbara in early Christian writings, in 1969 the Catholic Church declared her to be a non-historical person, and the Feast Day of St Barbara was removed from the General Roman Calendar. However, her name – and the brutal nature of her death – has since given the world the word 'barbaric', and her saintly status is still reflected in place names such as Santa Barbara in California.

St Lucia

In Sweden and many European countries, the beginning of Christmas festivities is marked by St Lucia, or Little Yule Day.

By tradition, early on the morning of Little Yule Day, whilst the family still sleeps, the eldest daughter awakes and dresses in a long white gown with a red sash. Wearing a crown of candles, she then proceeds to wake the family, serving them each with coffee and a St Lucia bun. Presuming the daughter doesn't accidentally burn down the house, she is then known as Lucia for the day.

With Lucia coming from the Latin word for light, the night of St Lucia – a celebration heralding the coming of light after the darkness of the long Scandinavian winter – was originally held on what was the longest night of the year: the winter solstice. With the introduction of the Gregorian calendar, the date of the winter solstice fell back to later in December, but Little Yule Day is still celebrated on 13 December.

Frau Holda

In Germanic folklore,
Frau Holda is the
goddess of women's
domestic chores and
childbirth. In particular,
the domestic goddess
is associated with the

spinning of yarn, as spinning was traditionally considered
both a woman's task and an important and time-consuming
skill before the arrival of the Industrial Revolution heralded
the mass production of cloth.

Portrayed as either a long-toothed,
crooked-nosed old hag…

…or a fair maiden dressed in white…

…the 'protector of the household'
is said to be all sweetness and light
until, woe betide the lazy offender, she
discovers an untidy house!

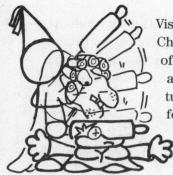

Visiting during the Twelve Days of Christmas to check on the spinning of yarn, Frau Holda will congratulate and reward a hard worker, but, in turn, a lazy worker will feel the full force of her sharpened tongue and rolling pin.

Frau Holda is also closely related to witches, the wilderness, wild animals and winter.

When it snows in the mountains of Germany, it is said that 'Holda is shaking out her feather pillows'. When there is fog, it is said to be 'smoke from her fire'; and when there is thunder, it is said that Holda is 'reeling in her flax'.

With her association with wilderness and weather, in the more remote parts of Germany festivals for Frau Holda are held in the middle of winter, usually on Christmas Eve or Twelfth Night, or for the entire Twelve Days of Christmas – the time when humans leave the mountains for the warmth of their home. During this time, the spinning of yarn is prohibited.

129

Frau Perchta

Similar to Frau Holda, Frau Perchta is Holda's southern cousin, the pagan domestic goddess of household chores, spinning and childbirth in the southern Germanic Alpine countries of Switzerland, Bavaria and Austria, and in the mountainous German region of Swabia.

Aside from sharing Holda's old hag or fair maiden looks, many see Perchta as also having one large foot. Sometimes called a goose or swan foot, the oversized plate of meat is thought to symbolise that Perchta is a higher being who can shape-shift to animal form.

Perchta is said to roam the countryside at midwinter, entering homes during the Twelve Days of Christmas.

Upon finding a sleeping child she believes to have been good, she will leave a small silver coin in their shoe. But, if she deems a sleeping child to have been bad, it is said that Frau Perchta will slit open the child's stomach, rip out their guts and fill the gap with rubbish.

From Perchta comes Perchten, painted wooden masks worn in parades and festivals on 6 January, the Feast Day of Frau Perchta.

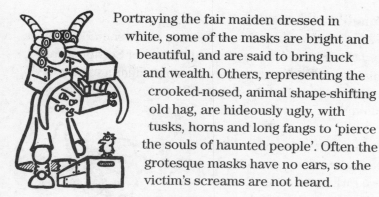

Portraying the fair maiden dressed in white, some of the masks are bright and beautiful, and are said to bring luck and wealth. Others, representing the crooked-nosed, animal shape-shifting old hag, are hideously ugly, with tusks, horns and long fangs to 'pierce the souls of haunted people'. Often the grotesque masks have no ears, so the victim's screams are not heard.

On the feast day, herring and dumplings are to be eaten. If herring and dumplings are not eaten, it is thought Frau Perchta will be further angered and will slit open a person's stomach, rip out their guts and fill the gap with rubbish; nothing, if not consistent.

Where Lucia takes her name from the Latin for light, Perchta, via the early German name of Bertcha, means 'the bright one', and it is from Bertcha that we arrive at the English name of Bertha. By all accounts, she may be all sweetness and light, but don't ever get on the wrong side of a Bertha!

Tomte, Nisse and Tonttu

A *tomte* in Sweden, *nisse* in Norway and Denmark, and *tonttu* in Finland, is a mythical creature of Scandinavian folklore. The creature comes not only under a variety of names, but a selection of guises.

Seen by some as an elderly, bushy-bearded farmer, somewhere between the height of a turkey and a roadside bollard…

…others believe the tomte-nisse-tonttu to be a shape-shifter, capable of appearing much larger than an adult; quite possibly as tall as a bus, and maybe even with a single, cyclopean eye.

Danish people picture a nisse as clean-shaven, dressed in red and grey knitwear and sporting a red cap; that is, when not invisible.

Norwegians see him as hairy all over, with pointy ears, four fingers and eyes that glow in the dark.

Whether big, small, hairy, cyclopean or not, it's generally agreed the tomte-nisse-tonttu is very strong.

Although welcomed as the guardian of a farmer's home and family, the mythical creature is easily insulted, and retribution can range from a mischievous prank to killing off the farmer's animals.

Appeasing the tomte comes in the form of gifts, in particular a bowl of porridge, left outside on Christmas Eve. If the Christmas porridge is not forthcoming, the tomte will either leave and be seen no more, or engage in pranks such as knotting the tails of the farmer's cows.

Chapter 19

CHRISTMAS CZECH-LIST

WHEN it comes to Christmas customs and traditions, folktales and legends, the Czech Republic deserves a chapter of its own...

To Have and Have Knot

To predict her future chances of tying the knot, an unmarried Czech woman must stand with her back to the door and toss one of her shoes over her shoulder. If the shoe lands with the heel facing away from the door, it is said she will soon marry.

Having established her future relationship status, an unmarried woman can then narrow down the location of her husband-to-be by shaking an elder tree. If the sound causes a dog to bark, it is said the man she is destined to marry lives in the direction from whence the dog can be heard.

Married or not, it is believed a pregnant woman can find out the sex of her baby based on the first visitor to enter the home on Christmas Eve.

Not so much forceps as forewarned.

Food for Thought
Czech farmers can ensure a successful year ahead by observing a few simple rules…

Christmas is a time for baking vanocka bread. Giving a piece of vanocka to cows on Christmas Eve will guarantee a plentiful supply of milk over the coming year.

Similarly, feeding vanocka to bees will ensure a bountiful supply of honey.

If a goat is given an apple on Christmas Eve, it will produce sugary-sweet milk.

Feeding peas, barley, wheat and poppy seeds to chickens on Christmas Eve will provide an endless supply of eggs.

Of Course…

When it comes to the all-important Christmas Eve meal, the people of the Czech Republic observe more customs and traditions than they serve courses…

It is believed a person who fasts for one whole day until the Christmas Eve dinner will see the 'golden piglet', a symbol of fortune.

There must be an even number of guests seated at the feast, as an odd number on Christmas Eve may bring, at best, bad luck; at worst, death.

No dinner guest should sit with their back to the door.

To protect the home from burglars over the year ahead, the legs of the table should be tied together with rope.

Placing a bowl of garlic under the table is thought to give strength and protection.

Placing fish scales either under the table cloth or dinner plates is thought to ensure a bright financial future for the family.

The home must remain in darkness until the first star appears in the evening sky, after which, dinner can be served.

The Christmas Eve feast must consist of nine courses. No alcohol must be served, and to leave the table before the end of the meal may bring, at best, bad luck; at worst, death.

After the final course, a guest at the table is called upon to cut an apple in half. If the core of the apple is star-shaped, it is thought that everyone at the table will have a happy and healthy year ahead, and will return the following year. If the core is revealed as a four-pointed cross, someone at the table will, at best…

The first person to leave the table after the Christmas Eve meal will be the first one to die, almost certainly within the following year. Guests must therefore all exit the table together.

Following the meal, no field must be crossed until after Midnight Mass. Once again, to do so will mean certain death in the year ahead.

The Future is Bright

Having hopefully survived the Christmas Eve feast and Midnight Mass, there are a number of Christmas customs in the Czech Republic associated with predicting the future over the coming year…

Upon cracking their Christmas nuts, each member of the family makes a small boat out of an empty half of a walnut shell. They then place a lit candle in the shell, and the shell into a bowl of water.

If the shell floats to the other side of the bowl, it is said they will live a healthy and long life. If the shell sinks, they will, at best…

A piece of lead is heated until it turns molten, and then poured into water. The shape made as the molten lead solidifies will suggest the pourer's destiny in the year ahead. Given the serious consequences of lead poisoning, I'd say, at best…

Section 6

OH, BRING US A FIGGY PUDDING

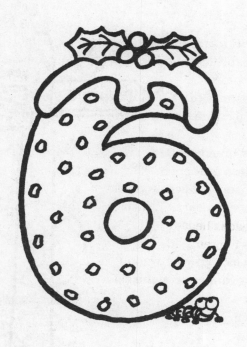

Chapter 20

GOD FEAST YE MERRY GENTLEMEN

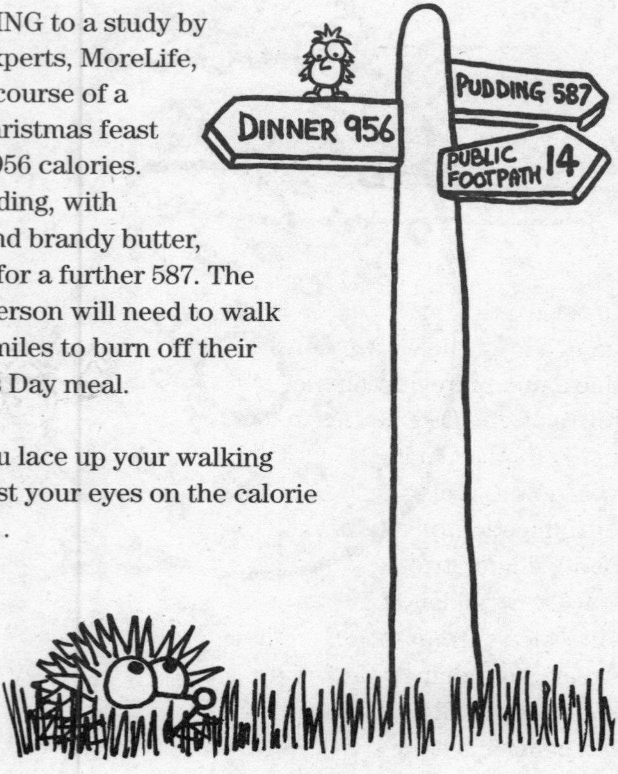

ACCORDING to a study by obesity experts, MoreLife, the main course of a typical Christmas feast contains 956 calories. Plum pudding, with custard and brandy butter, accounts for a further 587. The average person will need to walk fourteen miles to burn off their Christmas Day meal.

Before you lace up your walking boots, feast your eyes on the calorie counters...

DINNER 956

PUDDING 587

PUBLIC FOOTPATH 14

Turkey

There are a number of theories as
to how the turkey gained its name.
Perhaps the most suspect is that a
turkey's head bore an uncanny
resemblance to a Turkish
Empire soldier's helmet.

A further suggestion is that the
name came from the wild turkey's
'turk-turk-turk!' call, but if we
named animals after the sound
they made, our most popular
pets would be meows and
woofs, and we'd eat moos
and baas.

In reality, the turkey was incorrectly
named after the country Turkey
due a mix up regarding the
bird's origin. Originating, in fact,
in North and Central America, it
was domesticated in Mexico, and
introduced into Britain in 1526, care
of a William Strickland. On his
travels, Strickland bartered
six turkeys from Native
American Indian traders and
sold them in Bristol for two
old pence each.

By Victorian times turkey had become a popular Christmas dinner. With many birds raised in Norfolk, the turkeys were fitted with leather-soled sacking boots and walked the 100 miles to market in London.

Norfolk farmer, Bernard Matthews, introduced factory farming to Britain in the 1950s, making the luxury bird affordable to the masses.

And so, from its humble beginnings, the turkey has become the nation's favourite Yuletide dinner, with 10 million birds reduced to little more than bones each Christmas Day.

Weighing an average of 5.5kg each, that's the equivalent to eating the famed ocean liner, *Titanic*.

Goose

> *Christmas is coming,*
> *The goose is getting fat...*

Those who find turkey on the dry side might fancy a goose. Rich and fatty, it's best avoided if you have an aged relative with a heart condition coming to stay over the festive season, unless you stand to inherit a substantial sum of money upon their passing.

Wild Boar

Still popular in Scandinavian countries, in particular Sweden, the eating of ham at Christmas is thought to date back to Germanic paganism, when a boar's head would be served as a tribute to Freyr, the Norse god related to weather, farming and fertility.

Imported into England via the Anglo-Saxons, in medieval times a boar's head, with an apple wedged between its teeth, would be carried into the banqueting hall on a silver plate, accompanied by the sound of trumpets and singing minstrels; a tradition strangely not celebrated around the modern Christmas dinner table.

A more far-fetched story tells that the custom of serving a boar's head actually originated at The Queen's College, Oxford, after one of its students, walking in Shotover forest, was attacked by a wild boar. The student saved himself by wedging his *Logic of Aristotle* book down the animal's throat, whereupon the boar choked to death; the student removed the animal's head and returned, trophy under arm, to the college.

Swan

Many centuries ago, grand Christmas banquets could well involve a swan. In preparation, the bird's feathers and skin would be removed and the bare flesh painted with saffron dissolved in warmed butter. Following roasting and before serving, the skin and feathers would then be replaced.

Nut Roast

Where a turkey is dry, a wild boar or re-skinned swan is not available and a goose could well shorten your life expectancy, a nut roast offers endless possibilities – from walnuts to peanuts; mixed with sunflower seeds or bird seed; whatever tickles your taste buds.

Run by medical surgeon and famed cornflake creator, John Harvey Kellogg, in the early twentieth century the Battle Creek Sanitarium in the US state of Michigan included nut roast and cutlets on the menu. Aside from plenty of fresh air and enemas, Kellogg encouraged a low-fat diet rich with fibrous food and nuts.

One time guests at the sanitarium included car-maker Henry Ford, and on-screen Tarzan, Johnny Weissmuller.

Grab your nuts, add bread crumbs, chopped onion, garlic, mushrooms, a couple of eggs, butter and water, stir it all up and pop in the oven. Serve with apple sauce or rhubarb relish. Alternatively, buy pre-prepared from the supermarket. If there's only one vegetarian at the Christmas dinner table, your time may be better spent preparing the meat dish.

Angels on Horseback

Nothing to do with angels, or horses, angels on horseback are oysters wrapped in bacon; so named as when cooked the oysters curl up to resemble angel's wings.

If your budget won't stretch to oysters, or your local fresh fish shop is short on supply, you can replace the oysters with scallops. If you don't fancy scallops, replace the oysters with bacon, forget the garlic and parsley, and have yourself a juicy bacon butty.

What better way to start Christmas morning!

147

Devils on Horseback

If your budget won't stretch to oysters or scallops, or the family is not into fancy food, devils on horseback are a cheaper version of angels on horseback. Remove the stones from prunes, stuff with mango chutney, wrap in bacon and either grill or bake. If you've got a dodgy tummy, then replace the prunes with dates. If you don't fancy mango chutney, stuff with cheese, almonds or just about anything in the fridge that needs using up.

Pigs in Blankets

If there are kids in the family, forget the fancy oysters or healthy prunes, and opt for pigs in blankets – small sausages wrapped in bacon, grilled or baked. Make sure the sausages are pork; otherwise you'll have cows in blankets.

Stuffing

Take one large turkey and stuff with a goose, duck, mallard, guinea fowl, chicken, pheasant, partridge, pigeon and woodcock. Add an arm's length of sausage meat, a few rashers of streaky bacon and a bucket or two of sage, port and red wine stuffing, and you have a hearty Christmas feast for around 30 people.

Giblets

Take the heart, gizzard, liver and various other leftover 'giblets' from the Christmas feast creature of choice, and bake a delicious giblet pie.

A perfect Christmas treat for your pet of choice – unless, that is, you own a goldfish.

Brussels Sprouts

Brussels sprouts (note the capital B) gained their name when they first popped up out of the ground around the thirteenth century, in what is now Belgium.

Despite a 2002 survey citing the Brussels sprout as the most loathed vegetable in the United Kingdom, we produce over 160,000 tonnes of them every year, and very few are exported.

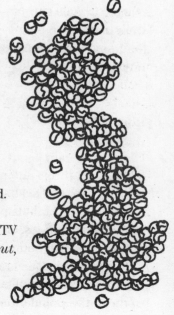

But, then, not all are eaten. In the UKTV food programme, *Sexing up the Sprout*, chef James Martin created a Brussels sprout ice cream and a Sproutini cocktail.

Ever present on the Christmas dinner plate, the sprout is packed full of vitamin C and high in fibre and sulforaphane, a chemical thought to reduce the risk of cancer.

The perfect sprout should be steamed for no more than seven minutes; boil it to within an inch of its life and the sulforaphane will emit a rather unpleasant sulphurous gassy smell, and several hours later you'll be passing wind like a sailor rounding Cape Horn.

Coincidentally, and possibly for that very reason, in 2009 sprouts were banned on board the Royal Navy warship, HMS *Bulwark*.

Roast Potatoes

Attacked by the Colorado potato beetle, tuber moth, potato aphid, leafhopper, thrips and mites, and susceptible to diseases such as powdery scab, leaf-roll, black leg and purple top, it's surprising the humble potato survives, let alone thrives.

But thrive it does.

Annual world potato production stands at over 330 million tonnes, equivalent to eating 1,102 Empire State Buildings, or somewhere approaching the combined weight of the entire population of the planet.

Originating in Peru several thousand
years ago, the potato has long been
part of Andean mountain
culture. The Incas believed
potatoes relieved the pains of
childbirth. Exactly how,
one can only imagine.

And to this day, it is
thought dragging a young
woman across a field will
bring fertility to the soil, ensuring
a successful potato harvest.

In the Andean mountain culture, potatoes are
also believed to hold the secret to future love
and fortune. Following another tradition,
in a large mound of mashed potato
are hidden a small coin, button, ring,
key, shell and heart-shaped charm.

With the darkened room, young
guests then search for the 'gems'.
The one who finds the small coin is thought
will gain wealth, whilst the key will bring success and
power. He or she who finds the button will remain a

bachelor or spinster, but the heart will bring love, and the finder of the ring will be the first to wed…

…Whilst the one who finds the shell will be travelling on a long journey.

Speaking of a long journey, following invasion and defeat of the Inca Empire, the Spanish introduced the potato to Europe in the second half of the sixteenth century.

Soon finding its way across the English Channel to Britain, the potato was at first treated with suspicion, with stories that it caused everything from lust to leprosy.

With no mention of the potato in the Bible, Scottish clergymen deemed the humble tuber unfit for consumption and banned their congregations from planting them. Although not on totally firm soil, the colloquial name

for the potato – spud – boils down from *spad*, the Latin for sword, via a number of other words for knives, daggers and digging tools, to the English spade, the very implement needed to dig the soil to plant the potato seeds.

The first food to be grown in space, aboard the space shuttle *Columbia* in 1995; whether on Earth or in orbit, served hot, cold, mashed, baked, boiled, fried, chipped or steamed, potatoes make a tasty meal. Roasted and covered in gravy, they earn a well-deserved place on the Christmas dinner plate.

Roasted Parsnips

It's commonly thought the parsnip gained its name from the coming together of parsley and turnip. Part correct with the 'nip', but the 'pars' comes from the Middle English 'pasnepe'.

In his writings of 1475, Italian Bartolomeo Platina noted that parsnips bring relief to dropsy, pleurisy and the common cough; they also arouse passion. Platina was not the first to be aroused by the root vegetable's health benefits: the Romans thought parsnips to be an aphrodisiac.

The spread of the Roman Empire brought with it the spread of parsnips to northern Europe, the Romans finding the further north they travelled, the bigger the parsnip would grow; and a parsnip can grow up to half a metre.

With a liking for frost and cold weather to develop their flavour, particularly in Ireland, the seeds and leaves were used to make beer and wine.

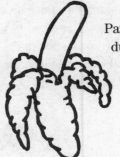

Parsnips also came into their own during the Second World War, mashed and mixed with banana flavouring to make imitation bananas.

Described as homely, old-fashioned and just slightly eccentric, the carrot's slightly dotty relative serves up well in stews, soups and casseroles, and roasted parsnip has earned its place as an essential part of the Christmas feast.

Bread Sauce

In the Henry James novel, *The Portrait of a Lady*, reasoning to her young American niece why England was not a desirable place to live, Lydia Touchett cites bread sauce. Bread sauce, in her opinion, had the appearance of a poultice and the taste of soap.

Originally a way to use up stale bread, bread sauce comes into its own once a year as the perfect accompaniment to the Christmas turkey.

Pick the green mould off the bread, reduce
it to crumbs, pop in a pot with some milk,
butter and fried onions. Add cloves,
nutmeg and bay leaves, then simmer
until it resembles congealed
porridge.

Cranberry Sauce

As the sound fades at the end of The Beatles' 'Strawberry
Fields Forever', John Lennon is heard to say 'cranberry
sauce'. Lennon's reference to cranberry sauce later inspired
the naming of Irish rock band, The Cranberry Saw Us, later
to find success as The Cranberries.

Aside from occasionally finding its way into a Brie
sandwich, cranberry sauce takes its place once a year on the
plate next to the Christmas turkey.

Take a punnet of cranberries, add
some sugar and boil in water until
they pop and the mixture
thickens. If you're feeling
exotic, then stir in some
maple syrup and a
squeeze of lemon. Good
for reducing blood
pressure, preventing
stomach ulcers, and
excellent for easing
cystitis.

Christmas Plum Pudding

Whether you have room or not after the 10-bird roast with all the trimmings, Christmas dinner is traditionally rounded off with plum pudding. Containing no plums, the pudding gained its name in the seventeenth century, a time when the word 'plums' was applied to raisins or other fruit.

Story tells that in 1714, King George I asked that plum pudding be served as part of his Christmas Day feast. For this he earned the unflattering title of 'Pudding King'.

Continuing a custom dating back to King George V, every December HM the Queen gives each of her staff a Christmas plum pudding.

By tradition, the best time to make plum pudding is Stir-Up-Sunday, the last Sunday before Advent. The day is so named as it is the day Church of England ministers call on their

congregations to be 'stirred up' and encouraged to perform good deeds. This leaves four to five weeks for the pudding to soak up the alcohol and the rich taste to mellow.

And rich it is. According to Christian tradition, plum pudding should have 13 ingredients: one to embody Jesus and one each for his 12 disciples. The ingredients include such strains on the heart as sugar, treacle, eggs, suet, dried fruits and spices; dark beers such as stout and porter; and, most importantly, brandy.

Once in the bowl, following the addition of some full fat milk, the batter should be stirred with a wooden spoon from east to west in honour of the Wise Men, who travelled to Bethlehem from the East.

To bring good luck over the coming year, every member of the family should take a turn in stirring the batter.

Before cooking, by tradition metal objects are added to the mix. These 'buried treasures' are said to predict the finder's fortune over the coming year.

A silver coin is thought to bring wealth, happiness and good health, whilst a ring will bring marriage.

If a single woman finds a sewing thimble, she will remain unmarried over the coming year.

When ready to cook, boil or steam the pudding for two to six hours, or pop in the pressure cooker for as long as it takes to knock back the remainder of the brandy and repeat 'Betty better butter Brad's bread'.

To serve, place a holly sprig on top, pour yet more brandy over and set alight. The holly is said to represent Christ's crown of thorns, whilst the brandy represents His passion.

Figgy Pudding

Not unlike Christmas plum pudding, only white and made with figs, figgy pudding comes into its own in the first chorus of the Christmas carol, 'We Wish You a Merry Christmas', where the singers repeatedly demand: 'Oh, bring us some figgy pudding'.

Bear this in mind next time carol singers come calling.

Brandy Butter

Take a very large knob of butter, a supermarket aisle of sugar, add a bottle of sherry and a few tots of brandy; give it a good stir, and what you have is brandy butter, a rich dessert sauce to accompany the flaming, brandy-soaked plum pudding.

Under European Union rules, to be labelled butter a dairy product requires a minimum of 75 per cent milk fat. Not only is brandy butter exempt from such Eurocracy, the traditional Christmas pudding accompaniment contains more than enough fat – milk or otherwise – to warrant a New Year gym membership.

Time to invest in a pair of elasticated-waist trousers!

Chapter 21

CHESTNUTS ROASTING ON AN OPEN FIRE

WHILST waiting 20 minutes to let the food go down, here are a few of the other things we enjoy eating at Christmas...

Mince Pies

In medieval times, due to a lack of winter feed for cattle, livestock would be slaughtered in the late autumn. The meat would then be encased in pastry, with dried fruits added, the sugar acting to preserve the meat and provide the family with food during the cold winter months.

In the eighteenth century, as techniques for preserving meat improved, the savoury element of the pie was gradually replaced, until all that was left was dried fruits.

160

And so was born the mince pie as we know it today.

In November 2011, a handmade mince pie went on display at the Marvellous Mince Pie Manufactory, a 'mince pie workshop' in The Exchange shopping centre in Ilford, east London. Using holy water from the French town of Lourdes to bind the pastry, the pie's ingredients included vintage Cognac brandy, ambergris sugar extracted from the secretions of a sperm whale, and vanilla beans and cinnamon from eastern spice markets. Before baking, a solid platinum coin was hidden inside, and the finished pie decorated with platinum leaf.

Valued at £3,000, the rich and tasteless offering was heralded as the most expensive mince pie in the world. A prize draw to win the 'luxury' pie was held a week before Christmas. Unless Mukund Soni, the six-year-old winner, had a taste for Cognac and sperm whale secretions, I imagine all but the platinum coin ended up in the bin.

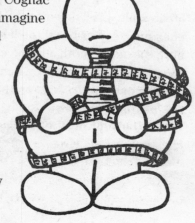

According to tradition, eating a mince pie on each of the Twelve Days of Christmas will bring happiness in the year ahead.

It may also warrant a January diet.

Roasted Chestnuts

Spare a thought for the humble chestnut tree. Whilst the sulphur-crested cockatoo carries out beak repairs on its branches, the grey squirrel strips its bark and the parasitic honey fungus rots its roots...

...polyfag moth larvae damage its shoots and foliage, oak leaf-mining moth larvae dig holes and deposit white spots on its leaves, and oak roller weevils roll up its leaves to protect their eggs.

Meanwhile, insects feast on the chestnut's flower buds, the larvae of both the acorn moth and the chestnut weevil set up home inside the nuts, and the oak aphid sucks on the tips of young shoots, whilst transmitting the chestnut mosaic virus.

If a sweet chestnut tree is not finished off by oak mildew, the grass grub beetle or ink disease attacking its roots and leading to dry rot, then there's sudden oak death.

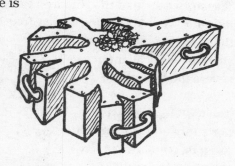

Surviving all of these predators, in the grounds of St Leonard's Church in Tortworth, south Gloucestershire, is a huge and ancient chestnut tree.

With multiple large trunks growing from the same roots, in 1720 the Great Chestnut of Tortworth was recorded as measuring over 15 metres in circumference at a height of 1.5 metres from the ground. The tree is thought to be more than 1,000 years old.

Somewhere between 2,000 and 4,000 years old, the Hundred Horse Chestnut, on the eastern slope of Mount Etna, is the oldest and largest chestnut tree in the world. With a circumference of 58 metres recorded in 1780, the tree is noted in the *Guinness Book of World Records* for having the greatest tree girth ever recorded.

The story goes that the Hundred Horse Chestnut gained its name when the young Queen Joan of Aragon, out on the slopes of the Sicilian volcano, was caught in a severe thunderstorm.

The Queen, along with her entire company of 100 Knights, were said to have sheltered under the tree.

Fast growing, the chestnut tree was the giant of ancient American forests, reaching heights of almost 60 metres. Before the arrival of chestnut blight in the early 1900s, in some parts of the States the chestnut tree accounted for one-quarter of all hardwoods. By 1940, the country's four billion chestnut trees had been reduced to barely enough wood to fuel a campfire.

The loss has been described as the world's greatest man-made ecological disaster.

In Europe, as the Roman Empire expanded north, chestnut trees were planted in mountainous areas where cereals struggled to grow. An important part of the Roman diet, soldiers would feast on sweet chestnut porridge before entering into battle.

The Romans also thought chestnuts offered protection against such things as mad dogs and dysentery.

In France the marron glacé, a sugar-coated chestnut, is traditionally served at Christmas, whilst on the island of Madeira, chestnuts are used to produce a fortified wine. If you don't care for a glass of Madeira, then fermenting the juice of a chestnut will produce a beer, whilst roasting the nuts can provide an after-Christmas dinner coffee substitute. For the health-conscious, chestnuts are less fattening than most other nuts and dried fruit, and they are the only nuts that contain vitamin C. But, be warned – too many chestnuts can give you a very bad case of wind!

Monkey Nuts
Come Christmas, the common peanut transforms into the monkey nut, left in its shell to be unwrapped in front of the fake log fire.

First grown in the coastal valleys of Peru around 7,600 years ago, the Incas entombed peanuts with their mummies to appease the gods.

No longer used as sacrificial offerings, with an annual global output of around 30 million tonnes, the number-one use for peanuts is peanut butter.

With more than 1,000 peanuts needed to produce a 700-g jar of peanut butter, there are enough peanuts grown in a piece of land the size of a tennis court to make 2,000 peanut butter sandwiches.

In 1929, a Bill Williams once used his nose to push a peanut to the top of Pikes Peak in Colorado. He reached the summit of the 4,302-metre mountain in 21 days.

Reaching an even greater height, in 1971, astronaut Alan Shepard took a peanut with him to the moon.

Dates

Partly dried, pitted and glazed with glucose syrup, a packet of sticky dates will often be found sitting on the Yuletide coffee table.

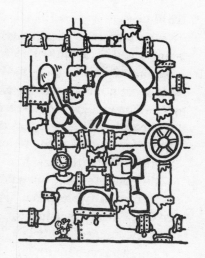

The fruit of the date palm, dates have found many uses throughout the world.

In Pakistan, the thick, sticky syrup is used to prevent pipes from leaking.

Soaked overnight in fresh goat's milk, ground and mixed with honey and cardamom powder, dates are thought to increase sexual stamina and endurance.

In traditional medicine, with its high tannin content, the 'cleansing power' of dates is used to relieve sore throats, colds, fever and hangovers, whilst in India the gum from a date palm's trunk is used to treat diarrhoea.

Yule Log

Now reduced to a short length of rolled-up chocolate sponge with a dusting of powdered 'snow', the Yule log was originally a whole hardwood tree, carried into the house with great pomp to provide warmth over the Twelve Days of Christmas. Keeping the charred remains of the Yule log throughout the year was thought to bring wealth and protection from evil, the remains then used the following Yuletide to light the new log.

The custom's roots are said to date back to sixth- and seventh-century paganism, with the Yule log burned on the eve of the winter solstice to mark the longest night.

Somewhat superstitious, story tells that Pagan log burnings excluded barefooted women, squinters and people with flat feet.

Celtic druids also lay claim to the burning of the Yule log, with an oak log symbolising life, and a pine log, death. After burning, the ashes were used to cure plant rust, swollen glands and 'animal complaints'.

Tangerines

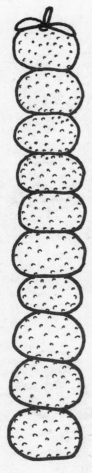

In answer to the proverbial question as to the difference between clementines, tangerines, satsumas and mandarins:

Clementines are small, seedless and easy to peel. It is said they are named after a Father Clément Rodier, who accidentally bred the hybrid orange at his orphanage in the Algerian town of Misserghin.

Tangerines, loose-skinned and less sweet, are named after the Moroccan port of Tangiers, from where they were first exported.

Satsumas, also with loose skins, come from the Japanese province of Satsuma, whilst mandarins, not greatly different in appearance from tangerines or satsumas, have been cultivated in China for around 3,000 years.

Confusingly, tangerines, clementines and satsumas are all types of mandarin, and – just to confuse things further – mandarins are often marketed as tangerines.

The custom of hiding a tangerine in a Christmas stocking originated in the twelfth century, when French nuns would leave socks full of tangerines, nuts and other fruit outside poor people's homes.

Chocolate Orange

Why eat a healthy tangerine when you can have a chocolate orange?

Although official figures are unconfirmed, it is quite possible that more chocolate oranges are sold at Christmas than there are planets in the entire universe.

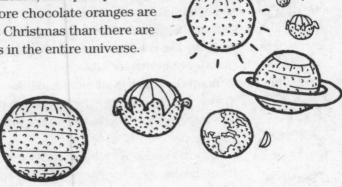

Hmmm, maybe not.

Chocolate Coins

With the United Kingdom part of the European Union, chocolate coins now come in both Sterling and Euros. Neither is legal tender, and – with bags of only a few chocolate pennies retailing at around £1 – they are also not especially good value for money.

Candy Canes

The most popular of Christmas sweets in the US, candy canes were straight white sticks of little more than solid sugar until, in 1670, a choirmaster at Cologne Cathedral in Germany was said to have had the ends bent to depict a shepherd's crook. The choirmaster would give the canes out to children at Christmas to both keep them quiet during church nativity plays and remind them of the part played by shepherds in the story of Christ's birth.

They didn't gain their red stripes until the twentieth century.

Chapter 22

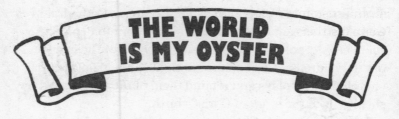

THE WORLD IS MY OYSTER

FROM oysters to putrefied skate, time to shake open the napkin and sample the delights of the Christmas feast around the world.

Argentina
Served on the night of Christmas Eve, a traditional Argentinean Christmas supper often includes peacock and stuffed tomatoes.

Australia
Christmas falling in the summer, the traditional Australian Christmas meal is said to be a 'barbie' on Bondi Beach, in the suburbs of Sydney.

Pity the Aussies who live 2,000 miles away in Perth.

Austria

For the customary Christmas feast, Austrians serve baked carp.

China

Although not great celebrators of Christmas, the Chinese do enjoy Peking duck and dumplings.

France

In the south of France, a special Christmas loaf is baked. Cut crosswise, the loaf is only eaten after the first slice has been given to a person who is without money.

Meanwhile, in Paris, oysters are considered a Christmas treat.

Greenland

Tasting similar to fresh coconut, a popular Christmas dish in Greenland is *muktuk*, the frozen skin and blubber of a bowhead whale.

For those not keen on whale blubber, an alternative dish is *kiviak*, the raw flesh of an Arctic auk bird. The flesh of the auk is first buried in seal skin for several months until it is in an advanced stage of decomposition.

Having polished off the whale blubber and decomposed auk, for pudding there is *suaasat*, a barbecued caribou soup with added berries and apples. Otherwise, with Greenland's long affinity with Denmark, you may just get a Danish pastry.

Popular presents in Greenland include sealskin mitts and a pair of tusks.

Iceland

The last day of the Catholic Christmas fast, the mass day of Thorláksmessa commemorates the death in 1193 of Thorlákur Thórhallsson, bishop of Skálholt and latter-day patron saint of Iceland. A public holiday, 23 December is the day for Icelandic people to buy last-minute Christmas presents, put up the Christmas tree and make final Yuletide preparations. It is also, by tradition, a day to eat skate.

Caught in Iceland's West Fjords in the late autumn, in preparation for Thorláksmessa the skate is pickled and then left to rot, until it gives off a strong and eye-watering smell of ammonia.

On the day of Thorláksmessa, the putrefied skate is served in chunks, alongside boiled potatoes and leaf-shaped bread, traditionally baked at Christmas.

Poland

In Poland, the Ukraine and many other Eastern European countries, the first course of the Christmas Eve supper is, by tradition, *kutia* – wheat or rice-based pudding, similar to porridge.

Before the meal, it is customary for the head of a farming family to toss a spoonful of *kutia* at the ceiling. It's believed the more it sticks, the more successful the harvest will be over the following year.

Russia

Christmas in Russia is mostly celebrated on 7 January, as the Russian Orthodox Church is still tied to the old Julian calendar.

For the strong of stomach, a popular Russian Christmas Eve supper may start with beetroot soup, accompanied by a cabbage and potato pie garnished with a gherkin salad, followed by a main course of sauerkraut and shredded carrot.

Ukraine

Traditional Ukrainian Christmas Eve celebrations begin with the Holy Supper, a 12-course meal, with each course dedicated to one of Christ's apostles.

In pagan times, ancestors were believed to be kindly spirits who, if shown respect, would bring good fortune. Consequently, the table for the Holy Supper is set with two tablecloths – one for the living, and one for the family ancestors.

Chapter 23

DING DONG! MERRILY ON HIGH

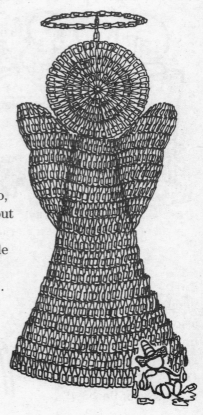

OVER five metres high
and nearly three metres
wide, the Christmas angel
displayed on Alfonso Reyes
Avenue in Monterrey, Mexico,
in the year 2000, was made out
of 2,946 beer bottles.

Time to crack open a bottle
and take a merry look at our
favourite Christmas tipples…

Sherry

Take a barrel of white wine, leave to ferment under a layer of yeast, stir in a few pints of a distilled grape spirit similar to brandy, and leave for three more years. The result – tasting not unlike cough mixture – is sherry,  a 'fortified wine' made from white grapes grown in the Sherry Triangle, part of the Spanish province of Cádiz.

 Intending to invade Britain, in 1587 the Spanish were preparing an armada off the shores of Cádiz. Gaining wind of their plans, English sea captain Francis Drake launched a pre-emptive attack, destroying the entire Spanish fleet. Drake returned to Britain with 2,900 barrels of sherry that were waiting to be loaded aboard Spanish ships. Thanks to his endeavours, sherry became a popular drink in Britain, in particular at Christmas.

Port

Similar to sherry, Port is also a fortified wine, usually produced from red grapes, grown exclusively in the Douro Valley in the northern provinces of Portugal.

Always spelled with a capital P, Port gained its name, not as an abbreviation of Portugal, but from the seaport of Oporto, from where Port is exported; exported, at first, thanks to the British.

Together with an alliance of European countries, in 1688 Britain began the Nine Years' War against France, and the British Navy immediately blockaded French ports. The blockade led in turn to a shortage of French wine, and so the British turned to Portugal for their wine supplies. With Portugal further away than France, shipping companies began adding the odd bucket of brandy to the wine in order to stabilise it on the long sea journey.

According to folklore, to speed up the process, the brandy was added earlier and earlier, until the Portuguese producers found adding brandy during the fermenting process stopped the wine's development whilst it was still sweet and fruity.

And, as an added bonus, it was a lot stronger.

Mulled Wine

A traditional winter warmer, mulled wine is red wine, heated and spiced with such delights as cloves, cinnamon, vanilla, ginger and sugar, served with a slice or two of fresh orange.

Often cheaper than normal supermarket wine, one suspects mulled wine may be produced using all the reject grapes not good enough to make it into a bona fide bottle of quality red.

Advocaat

Advocaat is said to have gained its name from the Dutch word *advocatenborrel*, used to describe a drink that lubricates the throat of a lawyer; hence the legal position of advocate, commonly referred to in English as a barrister.

But, then again, advocaat, as the name suggests, may have originally been an avocado-based liqueur produced in the former Dutch colony of Suriname in Latin America. Upon returning to the Netherlands, with avocados permanently out of season, the Dutch replaced the main ingredient with eggs.

And not just the odd egg: 10 egg yolks to one-and-a-half cups of brandy.

Stir in some sugar or honey, a drop or two of vanilla and a splodge of cream, simmer until the eggy smell rouses the

neighbours, and what you have is a rich and creamy liqueur about as appealing as a mushy pea cocktail.

As thick as lumpy custard, in the Netherlands advocaat is often eaten with a spoon – perfect as a waffle topping or in a pastry.

With an eye on increasing their profit margins, the canny Dutch then water down spare advocaat any for overseas export.

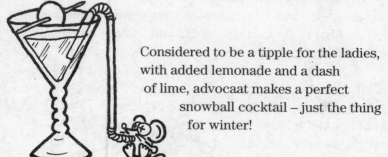

Considered to be a tipple for the ladies, with added lemonade and a dash of lime, advocaat makes a perfect snowball cocktail – just the thing for winter!

Eggnog

Christmas is the season for suspicious-looking yellow drinks, and there is none more suspicious than eggnog. Traditionally made with milk or cream, sugar, beaten eggs and either brandy, rum or whisky, the origin of the popular winter warmer is somewhat scrambled, although it's widely thought to have come from East Anglia, the nog a shortening of 'noggin', an old English word for a small hand-carved wooden mug used to serve alcohol.

Others believe eggnog came from 'egg-and-nog', a term often used in colonial America for rum and egg based drinks. Over time, egg-and-nog became egg-n-grog, eventually becoming eggnog.

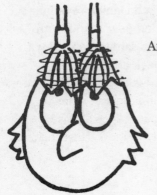

And the difference between advocaat and eggnog: advocaat is cooked, whereas eggnog uses fewer eggs and gets its creaminess from whipping the egg whites.

Julebryg Lager

Only on sale for 10 weeks of each year, Tuborg Julebryg is a special Christmas beer produced at the Carlsberg brewery in Copenhagen. Launched at exactly 8.59pm on the last Friday of October, on what is known nationally as J-Day, in a day of celebration Carlsberg employees drive around Denmark's bars and cafes handing out free beer. Revellers, in memory of a famous 1980 advertisement for Tuborg pilsner, dress in blue Santa costumes.

When not getting blue-Santa-costumed Danish revellers happily merry, Julebryg, a dark golden beer made from caramel malt and English liquorice, is said to go well with smoked fish, grilled herring, roast pork and duck.

RING OUT, SOLSTICE BELLS!

Chapter 24

BING BONG! MERRILY ON HIGH

AS WELCOME as hot mulled wine and a mince pie on a cold winter's night, Bing Crosby is guaranteed to lift the Christmas spirit...

'Silent Night'

The Great War; Christmas Eve, 1914; fighting in the trenches in northern France ceases and, in their respective  languages, the combined forces of Britain and France, together with opposing German soldiers, sing 'Silent Night'. Heavenly peace continues the next day, as the opposing teams famously play a game of football in 'No Man's Land'.

One of the most popular of Christmas carols, 'Silent Night' was written by an Austrian priest by the name of Joseph Mohr.

The story goes that Mohr was informed on Christmas Eve, 1818, that the organ at the Church of St Nikolaus in Oberndorf was broken. Not wishing a Christmas service without music, that day he sat and wrote the words, whilst the local headmaster, Franz Gruber, composed the guitar melody. Later that evening, 'Stille Nacht' had its debut performance in the small Austrian church.

The carol, once performed, was promptly forgotten, until an organ repairman discovered the lost manuscript in 1825.

It's a shame to pour cold water on a heart-warming story but, although the original manuscript of 'Silent Night' has been lost, a manuscript in Mohr's handwriting, dated by researchers as written around 1820, shows the priest actually wrote the words in 1816, when assigned to a pilgrim church in the Austrian village of Mariapfarr. Released as a single in 1928, Bing Crosby's version of 'Silent Night' sold over 10 million copies. Believing it wrong for a gambling person to profit from a holy song, Crosby donated all his royalties to charity.

'White Christmas'

In 1942, Bing Crosby starred in the film *Holiday Inn*, where he sang 'White Christmas'. Released as a single, the record has since sold over 50 million copies, the best-selling Christmas single of all time.

Just before 11am on 30 April 1975, American radio stations based in Saigon, the capital city of South Vietnam, announced that the temperature in Hanoi was 105 degrees and rising. The temperature check, followed by the playing of Crosby's 'White Christmas', was the coded signal for any US personnel remaining in the city to immediately make their way to Defence Attaché Office Headquarters for helicopter evacuation, bringing US involvement in the Vietnam War to an end.

'Jingle Bells'

Contrary to popular belief, the name of the horse in the song 'Jingle Bells' is not Bob, or Bobtail. 'Bobtail' refers to the horse's tail being cut short, or 'bobbed', as was commonly done to carriage horses to stop their tails getting caught in the carriage's reins.

Originally published under the title 'One Horse Open Sleigh', 'Jingle Bells' was composed in 1857 by American songwriter James Lord Pierpont.

The story goes that Pierpont was, at the time of writing, playing piano in Simpson Tavern, a former inn at 19 High Street, in the Massachusetts city of Medford. He was reputedly inspired by the town's popular sleigh races.

Trot ahead to 1943, and Bing Crosby recorded 'Jingle Bells' as a duet with The Andrews Sisters. The song galloped up the charts, selling more than one million copies.

Also selling over one million copies, in 1955 Don Charles recorded 'Jingle Bells' with nothing other than barking dogs.

One of the most performed and recognisable songs on Earth, 'Jingle Bells' lays claim to being the first song broadcast from Space, with the astronauts of *Gemini 6*, Tom Stafford and Wally Schirra, singing it on 16 December 1965, to the accompaniment of a miniature harmonica.

'The Little Drummer Boy'

Recounting the tale of a poor young boy who, unable to afford a gift for the baby Jesus, plays his drum for the newborn child, 'The Little Drummer Boy' is not exactly a lesson in how to get a baby off to sleep.

Made popular in 1958 by the Harry Simeone Chorale, Bing Crosby first recorded 'The Little Drummer Boy' in 1962.

He recorded it again in September 1977, as part of his upcoming *Merrie Olde Christmas* TV special, this time in duet with David Bowie. 'In duet' could be considered debatable, as Bowie instead sang 'Peace on Earth', written the afternoon before the recording of the show after Bowie expressed his dislike of 'The Little Drummer Boy'.

Crosby died the following month, but 'The Little Drummer Boy' / 'Peace on Earth' has gone on to become a perennial Christmas favourite.

Hark! The Herald Angels sing,
Glory to the long-gone Bing!

Chapter 25

DO THEY KNOW IT'S CHRISTMAS?

INTERVIEWED in 2010, Bob Geldof – the man behind supergroup Band Aid – declared in an Australian *Daily Telegraph* newspaper article that he considered himself responsible for two of the worst songs ever recorded: 'Do They Know It's Christmas?' and 'We Are the World'.

Anyone who has listened to the following Christmas songs may beg to differ...

'Please Daddy (Don't Get Drunk This Christmas)'
A seven-year-old boy asks his dad to go steady with the alcohol and avoid falling under the Christmas tree. Having penned 'Please Daddy (Don't Get Drunk This Christmas)', singer-songwriter John Denver was later arrested, suspected of driving whilst drunk. He should have, at the time, been arrested for penning quite possibly the worst Christmas record of all time!

'Christmas Conga'

Girls may want to have some fun, but little fun here as Cyndi Lauper surely wins a special award for rhyming longer, conga and bonga.

Could this be the worst ever Christmas songa?

'What Are We Going to Get For 'Er Indoors?'

Appearing on *Top of the Pops* in 1983, Dennis Waterman and George Cole – stars of TV series, *Minder* – pondered on how a coat made from skunk fur could be passed off to the wife as mink, taking into consideration that the coat had a tendency to 'pen 'n' ink'.

The Yuletide burnt offering reached number 21 in the charts.

'Grandma Got Run Over by a Reindeer'

Having drank too much eggnog and forgotten to take her medication, a grandmother stumbles outside into a snowstorm, where she is run over and killed by Santa Claus and his reindeer.

Putting a damper on the family Christmas, 'Grandma Got Run Over by a Reindeer' has continued to add to the annual pain caused by novelty Christmas music ever since.

Written by Randy Brooks, author of such classic songs as 'I'd Rather be Sailin' with Governor Palin' and 'It's Halloween (A Christmas Song)', 'Grandma Got Run Over by a Reindeer' was recorded in 1979 by married couple, Elmo Shropshire and Patsy Trigg. A year later, Elmo and Patsy divorced.

Unlike their marriage, each year the record went from strength to strength, until eventually, in 1984, it entered the US charts.

Although rumoured his ex-wife didn't actually take part in the original recording, Dr Elmo – a veterinarian by trade – unfortunately gave up his day job and went on to record a new version.

Nominated on multiple occasions as the worst Christmas song in history, as dire as it is, Dr Elmo has – and like the proverbial bad smell, is still having – had the last laugh, as 'Grandma Got Run Over by a Reindeer' has sold over 11 million copies, and – following the *Grandma Got Run Over by a Reindeer* TV Special in 2000 – become a best-selling singing-reindeer soft toy.

'Santa Claus Gave Me Diabetes'

On Christmas Day 2003, New York TV producer, writer and comedian Andy Stuckey discovered he had type 1 diabetes. Rather than keep his injections to himself, he teamed up with fellow TV producer and comedy partner Jon Murray to write and record 'Santa Claus Gave Me Diabetes', the song's lyrics laying the blame for his condition, somewhat undeservedly, on Santa Claus.

Having written a song with a line telling of how his girlfriend referred to him as 'Sweat Pea' due to the high sugar content in his urine, Stuckey has since declared a wish to one day form a band called The Dia-beatles.

Not quite blessed with the song-writing talents of John Lennon or Paul McCartney, perhaps The Dire-beatles might be more appropriate.

Chapter 26

DO THEY KNOW
IT'S CLIFF-MAS?

NOT COUNTING the odd line in Band Aid's 'Do They Know It's Christmas', Cliff Richard has topped the UK Christmas Singles chart three times.

Time to take a look at some other Christmas chart toppers...

The Beatles
Reaching the top of the charts in 1963, 1964, 1965 and 1967, The Beatles are the only artists to have had four UK Christmas number-one singles.

Spice Girls

With three consecutive Christmas number-one singles, the Spice Girls added flavour to the top of the charts from 1996–98.

Bohemian Rhapsody

Topping the charts on its release in 1975, and again in 1991 after the death of lead singer, Freddie Mercury, Queen's 'Bohemian Rhapsody' is the only record to reach number one in the Christmas Singles Chart on two separate occasions.

At the time of its release, music magazine *Melody Maker* likened Queen's showmanship to a frenzied performance of *The Pirates of Penzance* by the Balham Amateur Operatic Society.

Six minutes long and with no chorus, 'Bohemian Rhapsody' has gone on to become the

most played song on British radio after Procol Harum's 'A Whiter Shade of Pale'.

By coincidence, both 'Bohemian Rhapsody' and 'A Whiter Shade of Pale' contain the word 'fandango'.

'I Will Always Love You'

Featuring on the soundtrack to *The Bodyguard*, a film most notable for Kevin Costner's terrible haircut, Whitney Houston's 'I Will Always Love You' remained at the top of the Christmas 1992 chart for a record 10 weeks.

Popularly played to accompany a couple's first dance at their wedding, far from telling of the undying love of a newly married couple, 'I Will Always Love You' recounts the sad story of a woman who realises the man she loves is not right for her and she knows they must part.

Written by singer-songwriter Dolly Parton, Dolly's original version topped the US country music charts in 1974, and again in 1982, after appearing on the soundtrack to the film *The Best Little Whorehouse in Texas*.

Whilst Britain and the US were preparing to go to war with Iraq, in 2002 Saddam Hussein used 'I Will Always Love You' in TV and radio ads as part of his re-election campaign. Whitney Houston's record label filed a complaint with the Iraqi mission to the United Nations but, like Saddam Hussein's election opponent, it met with little success.

'Lily the Pink'

Based on the bawdy folk song, 'The Ballad of Lydia Pinkham', Scaffold's 'Lily the Pink' jollied its way to the Christmas number-one slot in 1968.

Noted as the inventor of medicinal compound, Lydia Pinkham was the nineteenth-century founder of a company selling a successful herbal 'women's tonic' intended to relieve menopausal and menstrual pains.

Traditionally sung post-match in rugby teams' changing rooms, during the Second World War, 'The Ballad of Lydia Pinkham' became the unofficial regimental song of the Royal Tank Corps.

Recorded at Abbey Road Studios in London, the backing vocals for 'Lily the Pink' were provided by Tim Rice and Reg Dwight. Whilst Reg Dwight changed his name to Elton John, Tim Rice – at the time a tea boy at the studio – went on to find fame as a lyricist for musicals such as *Jesus Christ Superstar* and *Evita*.

Further backing vocals were provided by Graham Nash, singer-songwriter with The Hollies, the line regarding Jennifer Eccles' terrible freckles being an in-joke referring to The Hollies' hit 'Jennifer Eccles'. Another in-joke pointing out Mr Frears' sticky-out ears referred to film director Stephen Frears, with whom Scaffold had earlier worked.

'Ernie (The Fastest Milkman in the West)'
Recounting the tale of milk delivery man, Ernie Price, and his fight with Teddington-based bread delivery and macaroon supplier 'Two-Ton' Ted to gain the love of Sue, a lonely widow from 22 Lindley Lane, comedian Benny Hill held the Christmas number-one slot for four weeks in 1971 with 'Ernie (The Fastest Milkman in the West)'.

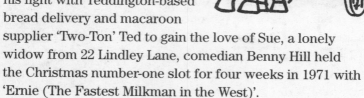

Hill wrote the hit song in 1955, the story inspired by his experience delivering milk for James Hann and Son (Dorset Dairies) in the Hampshire town of Eastleigh. The Market Street where Ernie is said to gallop runs through the centre of the town.

Interviewed on BBC Radio 4's *Desert Island Discs* in 2006, the Conservative Party leader David Cameron listed 'Ernie' as one of the favourite records of his childhood, admitting he often sang it at parties.

Whether that includes the Conservative Party…

'Merry Christmas Everybody'

Written by lead singer Noddy Holder and Jim Lea, the band's bass guitar player, Slade's 'Merry Christmas Everybody' shot straight to number one in December 1973, and remained in the charts until February of the following year. As perennial as mistletoe, 'Merry Christmas Everybody' has re-entered the charts on many occasions, and is often named as one of the UK's most popular Christmas songs.

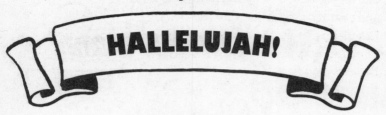

Chapter 27

HALLELUJAH!

CHRISTMAS is the time of year for choirs and choral societies to give a candlelit performance of Handel's *Messiah*. During the performance, it is customary for the audience to stand throughout the conclusion of the second movement, the 'Hallelujah Chorus'.

The tradition is said to have originated two centuries ago with London's first performance, attended by King George II. As the 'Hallelujah Chorus' began, the King stood, and remained so until the final note. Royal protocol demands that whenever the monarch stands so too does everyone in his presence, and thus the entire audience stood, initiating a ritual that has lasted to the present day.

Of the many explanations for the King rising to his feet at this point, it appears he may have suffered a touch of gout.

Chapter 28

LET THE GAMES BEGIN!

WHILST we're on our feet, time for some traditional English party games...

Hot Cockles
Nothing to do with fish food, and long before computer game consuls, Hot Cockles was a popular Christmas game in which one player would be blindfolded and the other players then took it in turns to strike the poor unfortunate.

Assuming the strike wasn't fatal, the struck person would then have to guess the name of the person who delivered the blow.

It's funny what passed for entertainment in medieval times...

Snapdragon

> *Take care you don't take too much,*
> *Be not greedy in your clutch,*
> *Snip, snap, dragon!*

From the sixteenth to the nineteenth centuries, the game of
Snapdragon was traditionally played on Christmas Eve.
A bowl of raisins soaked in brandy would be placed in the
centre of a table. Participants would gather around, the
room darkened, and the brandy lit.

The aim of the game was to pluck the burning, brandy-
soaked raisins out of the bowl, pop them in your mouth, and
'snap' your jaws closed to extinguish the flaming 'dragon'.

It was said the person who managed to pluck the greatest
number of burning raisins from the bowl would find their
true love within the coming year; quite possibly at the
Accident and Emergency department of the local hospital!

Cockfighting

Despite the name, there was no fowl play in this popular Victorian game.

Two players would lie on their backs, side by side, with feet pointing away from each other. Right arms were linked at the elbow, and right legs hooked together.

The winner was the one who could pull their opponent's heel over their head, causing them to perform a somersault.

Are You There, Moriarty?

A game dating back to late Victorian times, two players, first blindfolded, would lie face down, within close reach of each other, on the floor. Whilst grasping each other's left hand, in their right they would each hold a rolled-up newspaper. The first player would enquire: 'Are you there, Moriarty?' The second player would reply: Yes, Holmes, I am here'; and the first player would attempt to wallop him or her on the head as hard as he could.

The second player would then take his turn to do the same.

Why the game is named after Sherlock Holmes' archenemy, Professor Moriarty, is – not unlike one of Sir Arthur Conan Doyle's detective adventures – something of a mystery.

Reverend Crawley's Game

Somewhat the opposite to conducting a wedding service, the objective of Reverend Crawley's Game was to untie the knot.

The more participants the merrier would stand in a circle and link hands, but not with the person on either side, or both hands with the same person. The result was a giant human knot, and – without letting go of the hands they were holding – the knot had to be untied by crawling under arms, through legs and wherever one could go without risking a slap in the face.

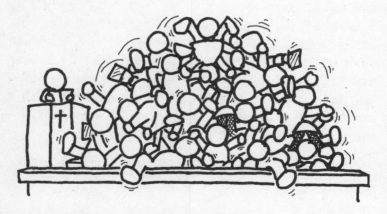

Exactly who Reverend Crawley was is a mystery, but he certainly knew how to keep his congregation entertained.

Section 8

MAIDS A-MILKING

Chapter 29

THE TWELVE DAYS OF CHRISTMAS

On the twelfth day of Christmas,
My true love sent to me...

Twelve Drummers Drumming

...represent the points of doctrine in the Apostles' Creed.

Eleven Pipers Piping

...represent the 11 apostles who remained faithful to Jesus.

Ten Lords a-Leaping

...represent the Ten Commandments.

Nine Ladies Dancing

...represent the nine choirs of angels.

Eight Maids a-Milking

...represent the eight beatitudes.

Seven Swans a-Swimming

...represent the
seven gifts of the
Holy Spirit.

Six Geese a-Laying

...represent the six days of creation.

Five Gold Rings
...represent the first five books of the Old Testament: Genesis, Exodus, Numbers, Leviticus and Deuteronomy.

Four Calling Birds
...represent the four Evangelists: Matthew, Mark, Luke and John, and the four gospels of the Bible.

Three French Hens
...represent the three theological virtues: Faith, Hope and Charity.

Two Turtle Doves
...represent the Old and New Testaments of the Bible.

And a Partridge in a Pear Tree
...represents Jesus Christ.

If you were to receive all of the gifts referred to in the 'Twelve Days of Christmas', you would receive 364 presents.

Chapter 30

ON THE FIRST DAY OF CHRISTMAS...

THERE is an old belief in Scotland that early on Christmas morning all bees will leave their hives, swarm and then return. Aside from this initial buzz of activity, Christmas Day in Scotland is generally a quiet affair.

With the Presbyterian churches regarding Christmas as a Catholic feast, following the Protestant Reformation of the sixteenth century, Christmas remained banned in Scotland for nearly 400 years. Meanwhile in 1647, English Parliament, under its new Puritan leader, Oliver Cromwell, decreed Christmas illegal. The ban was lifted in 1660.

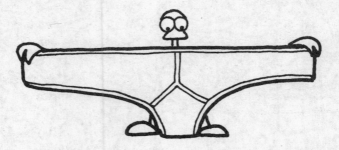

Since that day, in the UK the 12 days of Christmas have taken on the elasticity of a pair of well-worn underpants...

The First Noël

August Bank Holiday, two weeks before the kids go back to school. Step out of the late summer sun and into the supermarket to get some more charcoal for the barbecue. There it is, waving at you from Aisle 12: Christmas plum pudding.

Why would anyone want to buy a Christmas plum pudding in August? It's not as if you need to let it hang for weeks like a pheasant, or marinate in brandy for several months to bring out, the flavour before a final week's steaming the last bit of nutrition out of it in a pressure cooker.

The modern-day supermarket Christmas plum pudding needs around four minutes in a microwave oven.

In autumn 2009, Tesco frustrated shoppers by selling 'Santa's favourite' mince pies. Exactly how the supermarket giant discovered they were Santa's favourite is questionable, especially as the best-before date was 28 October, almost two full months before Santa would be squeezing his way down the chimney and sampling a bite.

Hoe! Hoe! Hoe!

September, and the day arrives to drop the precious little treasures off for their first day of the new school year.

Task done, you pop into your local Home and Garden DIY superstore to get yourself a new garden hoe. Something's different, but you're not quite…

And then you hear it, in between the announcements of the manager's special autumn discount on spring bulbs for the garden, radiating out from the overhead tannoy: Christmas music.

At least, you think what you hear is Christmas music, but you're not sure, as some of the notes have been changed to avoid music copyright infringement. As comedian Eric Morecambe famously pointed out when André Previn criticised his piano-playing abilities: he was playing all of the right notes, but maybe not in the order the composer had originally intended.

And the reason for this mangled festive music? Put down your hoe and wheel your trolley to the 'seasonal' aisle. Where last week they sold barbecues and garden furniture, there is now a glittering array of fake Christmas trees.

Why buy a real Christmas tree and spend until mid-April vacuuming up the last of the pine needles when your local Home and Garden DIY superstore will happily sell you a plastic one?

216

And a real Christmas tree isn't cheap: it costs an arm and a leg for one complete with roots and an unwritten guarantee the pine needles will remain in place longer than it takes to grow a Santa Claus beard. But, when Christmas is done and dusted, do you brave the winter weather and the frost to excavate a suitable hole for it in the garden?

And what if you move house?

In the midst of packing and taking old jigsaw puzzles to the charity shop and phoning solicitors, are you really going to go out and dig up the old Christmas tree?

Oh no! Buy a plastic one. Your Home and Garden DIY superstore will happily sell you any one of a number to suit your taste and pocket, from the size of a garden gnome complete with miniature baubles and twinkling lights…

…to a full-size replica of a giant sequoia with a string of lights longer than an airport runway…

217

…in a full range of colours. Why stick to the traditional green tree when you can have anything from pink with yellow spots, to something that looks like it may have been made from the floor sweepings of a local barber's shop?

And if you're concerned about the environment and the use of non-renewable plastic, then buy an alternative fake tree made of paper or card, or glass or aluminium, or even a holographic tree.

And why get one the right way up, when you can get an upside-down tree, leaving more space to store the presents?

Unless there's a miracle development between Mother Nature and plant scientists, you won't ever get a real upside-down tree, and the Home and Garden DIY superstore is having an end-of-summer sale on all Christmas trees. It could be time to get out the plastic.

A Ray of Hope

For sale alongside the fake trees – a glittering array of fairy tree lights. No more of the dim old lights with their replacement bulbs. No more having to replace every bulb in turn to work out which one has blown.

You see the light. LEDs! A five-metre string of bright bulbs that last forever and ever, and, even if they don't, when one bulb blows they still keep working. And they still keep working in white … or red … or blue…

And you can have them on in endless settings: on … off … on … off, like the blink of a car indicator, or fade on … fade off … flicker, flicker, flicker … strobe, strobe, strobe…

Christmas Comes But Twice a Year

October, and Christmas is firmly under way. Why not treat yourself to a 'Turkey and Tinsel Weekend' at a British seaside holiday camp?

Arrive on the Friday for Christmas Eve festivities, followed by Christmas Day, with crackers, party hats, turkey dinner with all the trimmings and a jolly old knees-up in the

OF COURSE, IN MY DAY…

evening, then have someone else serve you up the bubble-and-squeak leftovers on Sunday Boxing Day.

No need to invite the family for the usual Christmas Day arguments, or listen to a relative releasing excess wind as he or she reminisces about past Christmases and how they coped with food rationing during the war.

Get it all over and done with early and free up your time for the end-of-year Christmas sales.

Good King Wenceslas Looked Out...

Nine weeks to go, and there are carol singers at the door.

'Carol singers?! It's not even Halloween!'

'But, we're raising money for the local...'

'Yes, of course you are. And is that your dad lurking in the bushes?'

'Well, mum said, you can't be too careful nowadays, and we should go out before the clocks change.'

Let There Be Light!

The last Sunday in October, the clocks have gone back an hour and it's dark by mid-afternoon: time to put up the outdoor Christmas decorations.
It all started with a few twinkling lights – just enough to show the neighbours you were embracing the Christmas spirit. But then, each

year came a few more. Five metres became 10; 10 became 20. And 20 became multi-streams of blue snow twinkling as it cascaded down from every window. Then the illuminated Santa on his sleigh, complete with all nine reindeer, Rudolph with his red nose shining bright; and snowmen, and elves, and icicles, and...

To You and Your Family

November, and already one or two Christmas cards have dropped through the letter box; always from the distant and aged relatives who like to ensure they don't miss the last posting date.

On the back, the cards say the name of a charity, and on the front, pictures of robins and snow scenes and wreaths on doors of picturesque snow-covered cottages. Inside, messages that read 'To you and your family', as the sender can't remember the names of your children.

Why?

'Family' pubs have rediscovered the letter 'Y', as large signs
with red and gold lettering begin to appear announcing
'Christmas Fayre', in the hope that you'll be tempted inside
by the offer of ye goode olde medieval banquet of boar's
head served on a silver platter with all the trimmings; a
three-course meal-deal, including a free goblet of mead.

Sadly, due to the lack of a slowly rotating hog roast close
to the designated smokers' area in the car park, you suspect
overly dry turkey and a nut roast for the vegetarians is
more likely to be found under the laminated plastic of the
'specials' menu.

eTail Therapy

Six weeks to go before the big
day; time for some Christmas
e-shopping.

Oh, joy! Everything delivered to your door without the
hassle of having to weave around crowds of slow-moving

shoppers laden with bags; or overweight shoppers who waddle from side to side like a giant counterbalance to stop them falling over, knowing that regaining an upright position could well involve a paramedic. And women struggling with double-buggies that barely fit through shop doors, or three-wheeled buggies with giant inflatable tractor tyres.

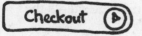

No more standing in long queues; or having to sit in endless traffic to get to the shopping centre, only to then wait in another long queue for the multi-storey car park, where the only space available is on the exposed-to-the-elements roof. And, chances are, you have to walk down a floor to get to the one working lift, down a bare concrete stairwell that smells of stale urine; a lift that appears to gain pleasure from stopping at every single floor.

Dispatch

Checkout ▶

Internet shopping, it's what the credit card was invented for.

Once in Royal David's City Centre

The original Santa Claus, Saint Nicholas of Myra, was, amongst many other things, the patron saint of pawnbrokers.

Talking of pawnbrokers, with five weeks until the big day, having done the bulk of your present buying online, it's time to add to the mounting credit card debt at the shopping centre. You tell

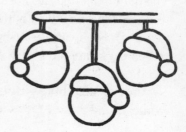

yourself it'll be the only visit, and you'll be done and home in two hours, but you know in your mind you'll be there all day, and it will be the first of many visits.

In the lift down from the multi-storey, you consult your mental shopping list: body scrub, music voucher, chocolate orange, one-metre long Toblerone, birthday cards for Noah and Holly...

Support tights, gold marker pen, party poppers, sexy underwear!

According to a survey by laundry specialist, Dr Beckmann, of the 24 million pairs of knickers bought as a Christmas present by UK men each year, 12 million will never grace their partner's buttocks. Either they are deemed too racy, too lacy or, in the case of 31 per cent, they are simply the wrong size – the wrong size being nearly always too small.

Spray snow, lottery ticket, chocolate money... cashpoint!

Out of the lift, and the queue for the cashpoint is longer than the queue outside the Post Office on pensions' day. Why is there always a queue at the cashpoint when everyone pays with their credit card?!

And so, eight hours, three Xmas Blend skinny lattes and a

cheeseburger meal-deal later, weighed down with boy-band calendars, DVD boxed sets, knitted toe-socks; an inflatable chef's costume, flashing novelty tie, chocolate calculator; *The Best of Pan Pipes volume 3* double CD, four candles and various other 'Secret Santa' presents, you eventually make it home, exhausted.

You've Got Mail!

Back home, kettle on, quick check of your emails: Christmas offers!!! You try to unsubscribe, but first you have to click on 'show content'. But you don't want to click on 'show content' as you're annoyed at getting the email in the first place. And if you 'show content' your computer will then ask if you want to 'add contact', and before you know it, you'll be a friend of a giant supermarket chain on Facebook, receiving regular status updates on their frozen turkeys and Buy-One-Get-One-Free offers.

Santa's Favourite Mince Pies

Buy one – Get one free!

Why can't they just BOGOF!

Oh Come, All Ye Faithful

One month to go and you can't put the decision off any longer. The family has been asking for weeks what your

Christmas plans are. Are you coming to them, or would you like them to come to you for a change? How about we stay here, and you stay there for a change?

They say they don't mind sleeping on the inflatable mattress, but you know you'll have to give up your own bed.

And what about the in-laws? They've invited you to their house on Christmas Day but it's a bit of a drive and little Johnny gets car sick. And one of you can't drink as you have to get back as the kids are going to the ex on Boxing Day.

According to a survey for car insurance company, Allianz Your Cover, 42 per cent of people said their Christmas had been ruined by an argument in the car.

A survey by IT company Buffalo LinkStation also reported that more family arguments are caused by who has control of the TV remote on Christmas Day than anything else.

Oh, the nightmare! You don't want your Christmas ruined.

Why can't you just spend it at home – open the presents, cook a nice meal, watch the Queen's Speech, play a few games and relax with a nice glass or three of eggnog?

I Gave at the Office

Four weeks to go; it may still be November, but it's time for the long-awaited office Christmas party. A few words of warning:

Novelty Christmas underwear, adorned with the likes of 'Ho! Ho! Ho! Santa's coming!' is best kept out of sight at all times. That is including, in particular, at the office Christmas party. Once the free alcohol has kicked in and you've sat your naked bottom on the photocopier, do not under any circumstance think that, whilst they are around your ankles, it would be very funny to return to the party wearing your novelty Christmas underwear on top of your dress, skirt or trousers.

Likewise, if you are a man, unless it specifically states 'fancy dress' on the invite, it's best not to wear a dress or skirt. It's also best not to wear a flashing bow tie, Santa Claus costume or Rudolph the Reindeer hand-knitted Christmas jumper.

Try not to dance like a funky chicken. And try not to dance like your father at a wedding. It takes time to develop such a skilful lack of coordinated body movement.

227

If you have a moustache or beard, before going to the party shave it off. Everyone will comment on how much younger you look.

Don't wear your hair in a comb-over.

Bald or otherwise, ponytails are no longer in fashion. And turn down the collar of your shirt; we're no longer in the 1980s.

If you're middle-aged, that single earring is doing you no favours.

As a woman, don't ask the barman for eggnog; if the music is loud, eggnog and snog can easily be confused.

Try not to return from the toilet with your dress or skirt accidentally tucked into the back of your underwear; especially if wearing a thong.

Male or female, remember an office romance is a dangerous thing, especially if one or both of you have a ring on your finger.

According to a survey by restaurant chain T.G.I. Friday's, 19 per cent of staff will embarrass themselves at their office Christmas party, with one in four staff admitting to romantically kissing one of their fellow workers. The worst department is thought to be Human Resources, with 55 per cent admitting to sharing a romantic kiss.

A further survey found workers in the travel and leisure industry are most likely to remove their clothes, with one in ten admitting flashing 'private' body parts, whilst one-third of workers in PR and the media confess to having at one time ended up in bed, post-party, with a co-worker.

Market Research

Three weeks to go and you're off out again. This time, to the market.

Except that the local market square that normally sells cheap batteries and brightly coloured tracksuits has long since been given over to small wooden sheds and been re-designated a Christmas market, each shed with a small battery radio playing a different Christmas song; the cowbell-cacophony drowning out both the sound of the local church bells and the gathering of jolly carol singers with their yellow charity collecting buckets.

Hot mulled wine is on sale in plastic beakers at 'only' £3.50 a cup; and the market is so crowded with Christmas shoppers you'd think you were taking part in a world record attempt at seeing how many people you can squeeze inside a Mini; only someone forgot to bring the Mini.

And the 'chalets' sell everything from hand-knitted reindeer jumpers to everything you'd expect from a normal craft market, most of which will soon find its way, post-Christmas, to a charity shop.

With all the money changing hands, one suspects it won't be long before a supermarket chain moves in and the sheds will be fitted out with self-service (or in this case, elf-service) checkouts. And batteries will be on offer, 'Buy nine volts, get an extra two free'…

For My Wonderful Goddaughter's Pet Cat Tiddles
Two weeks to go; time to pay a quick visit to Kards-R-Us.
Racks and racks of cards to suit everyone's pocket and taste:

'To My Gorgeous Girlfriend – I
Love You!' So big you'll struggle
to get through the doors of
the bus.

Colour-Your-Own (and buy
your own crayons).

Buy-Two-Get-One-Free
multipacks that ensure you'll
have plenty of cards left for
the following year; except you
won't be able to find them the
following year...

...with price codes like AA, RAC and ABBA; codes aimed to
confuse so you don't realise you've quite possibly paid more
for the card than the present.

Catering for every eventuality, the racks of cards grow
longer by the year:

'To a Wonderful Niece and her Boyfriend'...

'To a Special Doctor'...

'A Christmas Message, Vicar'...

'A Special Christmas Message from Sir Cliff Richard'...

And then there's the problem that the family is no longer a family since Dad went off with the woman he met at the office party; the one he spotted with her skirt accidentally tucked into the back of her knickers. And Mum has since remarried.

But luck is in...

'For Mum and Her New Husband'...

'To My Dad and Stepmum'...

'To My ex-Mother-in-Law'...

Cards with turkeys and cutesy kittens Photoshopped with Christmas hats; Santa Claus urinating down a chimney, with the 'joke' line, 'No, I said Wii!'; cards with tinny music that you can't put back on the shelf quickly enough; endless jokes based on Brussels sprouts and flatulence...

...And, to top it all, cards for your pet. Why would any sane person buy a card for their pet? Your cat may appear more intelligent than certain members of the family, but it still can't read.

A quick visit to the card shop? I don't think so.

Please Mr Postman...
Returning home and, just as you arrive at the front door, the postal operative cycles up, barely able to turn the corner and three hours late for their daily delivery as they're weighed down with all the extra Christmas mail. Extra Christmas mail, and you've only just bought your cards, let alone written them.

AND HE'S STILL WEARING SHORTS!

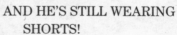

It's mid-December, you're wrapped up like you're off to spend winter in Siberia, and the postal operative is still wearing shorts, whistling away and happy as a pig in muck. If it's not all the overtime and imminent Christmas bonus, then someone's been putting something in his tea.

Bin and Gone

Having made small talk and signed for the latest parcel delivery, you drop the bags inside the door and then return to wheel the empty bin in. The local council waste-disposal operatives have kindly left a leaflet under the lid listing where you can recycle your Christmas tree, even though you haven't yet bought your Christmas tree!

More of a worry, the next bin-emptying day will be on Christmas Day, and there's more likelihood of seeing a flying pig in a Santa costume on Christmas Day than there is of seeing a council waste-disposal operative.

You could just put the bin out on Christmas Eve, knowing that at some point over the following days (usually around 5am in the morning) the yellow flashing lights and whirring, beeping and crunching sounds will signal that the waste-disposal operatives are going about their business.

But you don't want to leave the bin out on the off-chance, as you're going away for a few days and – even though you have one of those fake burglar alarm boxes on the front of the house and you always leave lights on timers to fool people into thinking you're in – the burglars will know by the bin sitting outside, the house is empty.

Away in a Manger
Ten days to go, and tonight is the long-awaited night; at least, for your child. After weeks and weeks of rehearsing the line, 'And then the three wise men arrived on their donkeys', it is, finally, the evening of the school nativity.

Only time for a quick piece of toast as you have to get to the school early so your budding little actor has plenty of time to get into his costume; the costume you so lovingly made from old pyjamas and a tea cloth.

You struggle to find a place in the car park amidst the other parents' 4x4s and people carriers. And the hall is, as always, cold. But at least the cost of the ticket includes a free glass of mulled wine, albeit in a plastic cup.

And then you sit for two hours, as an entire school of children wearing papier-mâché angel wings and assorted other dubious homemade costumes take it in turns to gather around a plastic doll Jesus, until, at last, you hear the immortal words...

'And, then ... the ...three ... wise ... donkeys...'

Return to Sender

Five days to go until Christmas, and tomorrow is the last possible day for sending first-class post. You've got to get those cards written. You promised yourself last year you'd be more organised. If you'd sent them last week you could have used second-class stamps. And you're not sure whether some of the cards count as 'large letters', so you're going to have to go and queue up in the Post Office.

You Shall Go to the Ball!

Only two days to go!

'Why did you book tickets for the pantomime so close to Christmas Day?'
'It wasn't me who booked them!'
'Oh yes, you did!'
'Oh no, I didn't!'

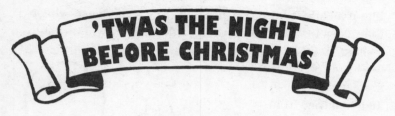

Chapter 31

'TWAS THE NIGHT BEFORE CHRISTMAS

ACCORDING to folklore, bread baked on the Eve of Christmas will not go mouldy. Perhaps not before the Twelfth Night, but after that I wouldn't recommend using it for the kids' packed lunches.

Also, rather thinly sliced in the truth department, in Belgium it is said to be illegal to throw bananas at police cars on Christmas Eve.

In eastern Poland, it is thought if a young woman grinds poppy seeds on the Eve of Christmas, she will marry within the coming year.

Christmas Spirit

In most countries, to be born on the Eve of Christmas is considered lucky. Not so lucky in Greece, where it's said that if a child is born on Christmas Eve, every year, whilst they sleep on the night of their birthday, they will turn into a ghost.

To avoid this, from 11pm on Christmas Eve, until the first crowing of a cock on Christmas morning, they must count the holes in a sieve.

Err on a G-String

And so, we arrive at Christmas Eve. Known to retailers as Desperado Day, it's the day that – having once again left it to the last minute – men desperately rush to do their Christmas shopping. The single busiest shopping hour of the year is said to be between 3pm and 4pm on Christmas Eve.

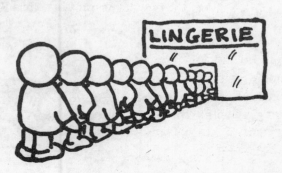

Dashing Through the Snow...

Whilst men shop till they drop and radio stations play all the perennial Christmas favourites, mince pies and cakes have to be baked.

Despite being the one day of the year that it's possible to bake everlasting, never-to-go-mouldy bread, the supermarket own-brand white loaf will have to do, as last-minute presents not only need wrapping, but also buying.

Oven Ready

And once the mince pies and cakes have had their turn, the turkey has to be stuffed and in the oven by 4 o'clock, in order – with a cooking time of 30 minutes per kilogram and an hour on top for good measure – to be ready for the next day's ceremonial reduction to a bare carcass.

Not, of course, that the turkey will fit in the oven without being beaten into the shape of a cube.

Don't Panic! Don't Panic!

And so, whilst Santa is busily rushing around at 671 miles per second, so are you…

Cleaning the bathroom…

…and vacuuming and dusting before the family arrives.

Meanwhile, the kids want to go to the park to re-enact a game of Christmas Day, 1914 No Man's Land football with their German school friends…

…but the dog needs a bath…

…and the ashen faggots need to be prepared…

…and friends are coming around early evening for a pre-Christmas mince pie, mulled wine and a round or two of Reverend Crawley's Game.

In amongst it all, the family phones once again just to check what time they're expected, and to ask if there's anything they

can bring. Even though you say no, you know they'll bring half a box of Christmas crackers left from last year, a tin of individually wrapped chocolates, three dozen homemade mince pies and, quite possibly, several jars of pickled onions, pickled beetroot, or anything else even vaguely pickle-able.

And, of course, a poinsettia. They always bring a poinsettia!

Oh, and a TV listings guide with everything circled that they want to watch this side of New Year's Eve; and they only stopped at New Year's Eve as they were so far through the magazine they'd started highlighting the furniture sale adverts.

Then the smoke detector outside the kitchen goes off…

And, before you know it, it's nearly midnight. The day is gone, it's time for bed, but… 'Quick everyone, shoes on, we're late for Midnight Mass!'

In Poland, on the way to Midnight Mass, it is traditional for single young women, having first blindfolded each other, to attempt to touch a picket fence.

If the fence is found to be straight and smooth, it is said their future husband will be smart and quick-witted, whilst a tumbledown old fence is a sign that he will be not quite so smart and practical.

All Kneel

Christmas Eve, and twelve of the clock,
'Now they are all on their knees,'
An elder said as we sat in a flock
By the embers in hearthside ease.

First published on Christmas Eve, 1915, Thomas Hardy's poem, *The Oxen*, recounts the belief that, in respect to the birth of Jesus Christ, at the stroke of midnight on the Eve of Christmas, all farm animals kneel.

245

Should you, at that moment, come across a kneeling donkey, it is believed that making the sign of the cross on its back will bring you what you most desire.

Bees, meanwhile, on the stroke of midnight, are thought to hum Psalm 100, giving thanks to the Lord.

Animals are also, at that very moment, able to speak; but for a human to hear their conversation is considered fatally unlucky.

This may not be so bad if you live in Ireland, as heaven's gates are said to open at midnight on the Eve of Christmas, and those who pass away before the gates close will be admitted without having to wait for Purgatory.

Find the Pickle

Before finally going to bed, it is considered traditional in
Germany for a member of the family to hide a glass pickle in
amongst the branches of the Christmas tree. On Christmas
morning, the first member of the family to find the pickle
will have good luck over the coming year.

This is, in reality, not an age-old custom at all, and
Germans appear mystified as to the legend's origins.

Chapter 32

WE WISH YOU A MERRY CHRISTMAS

AT LAST, it's Christmas Day!

Although snow may be falling over many parts of the country, it is commonly said that a white Christmas in England is marked by a single snowflake falling on the roof of the London Weather Centre on Christmas Day. Were this true, England only had seven official white Christmases during the entire twentieth century.

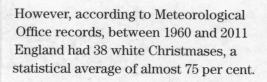

However, according to Meteorological Office records, between 1960 and 2011 England had 38 white Christmases, a statistical average of almost 75 per cent.

It is thought that hearing a cricket chirp on Christmas Day will bring good luck.

It is also said that sneezing on Christmas Day will bring good luck. Just be careful not to do it at the breakfast table!

A Bone of Contention

According to a lifestyle management study, during the final week of December an average of 10 hours are spent arguing with the family on the subject of Christmas. Due to the excitement and stress, it's been calculated that the first row will begin at precisely 9.58am on Christmas Day.

You may, at this time, be about to enter church. In Britain, the Holy Days and Fasting Days Act of 1551 dictated that every citizen must attend a Christian church service on Christmas Day. Well before the invention of the motor car, the Act further forbade the use of any kind of vehicle to travel to the service.

249

Although the Holy Days and Fasting Days Act of 1551 was abolished by Section 1 of the Statute Law (Repeals) Act of 1969, Section 1 of the Statute Law (Repeals) Act of 1969 was, in turn, repealed by the Statute Law (Repeals) Act of 1998, leaving the question as to whether, in Britain, every citizen must by law attend a Christian church service on Christmas Day (without the assistance of any kind of vehicle) up for debate.

If you do make it to church, it is believed the first person to enter the house on returning from church on Christmas Day morning will experience bad luck, possibly even death!

A Christmas Porky Pie

You may, however, in (or not in) contravention of the Holy Days and Fasting Days Act of 1551, remain at home to cook the Christmas dinner.

Rather more suspect than an undercooked turkey, story tells of a medieval English Christmas banquet, the centrepiece of which was a giant pie. Reputedly nearly three metres in diameter, the pie

was said to consist of 'two bushels of flour, twenty pounds of butter, four geese, two rabbits, four wild ducks, two woodcocks, six snipes, four partridges, two curlews, six pigeons and seven blackbirds'.

I Saw Mommy Kissing Santa Claus

So, the kids woke you up early to inform you that Santa had paid a visit, ate the mince pie, drank the traditional sherry, pocketed the carrot for Rudolph, and went on his merry way.

364 presents have been opened.

The Holy Days and Fasting Days Act of 1551 has again, quite possibly, been broken.

Party poppers have been popped.

You've pulled the Christmas cracker.

You've had your fortune read by way of a very thin plastic fish.

Dinner has been eaten.

Pudding has been served.

The dishwasher has been loaded.

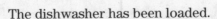

252

A single snowflake has yet to fall on the roof of the London Weather Centre.

You're wearing your novelty Christmas clothing.

Arguments have been had.

Alcohol has been drunk.

The kids have watched *The Wizard of Oz* whilst Granddad snored gently in the armchair...

253

The King's Speech

…And, before you know it, it's 3 o'clock – time for a nice cup of tea and the Queen's Christmas Address to the Nation, otherwise known as the Queen's Speech.

The first Christmas Address to the Nation was made via radio by King George V in 1932. The King's Speech was written by Rudyard Kipling, most celebrated as author of *The Jungle Book*.

Shake, Rattle and Roll

An afternoon of board games…

…and computer games…

More eating.

More drinking.

More arguments.

The Snowman.

Bumper episodes of TV soaps…

…and *The Two Ronnies* Christmas special…

And before you know it, it's goodnight from Santa. Christmas Day is over, and it's time for the inflatable mattress.

Looking on the bright side, it's estimated a normal double mattress is home to up to 10 million dust mites. As an inflatable mattress is deflated after use and stored away, it doesn't accumulate months of a sleeping person's dead skin cells for mites to live on, so at least you won't have them nibbling at you all night long!

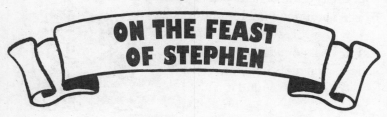

Chapter 33

ON THE FEAST
OF STEPHEN

WAKING up on a partly deflated inflatable mattress, we arrive at 26 December: Boxing Day.

No one is exactly sure how Boxing Day gained its name. Officially St Stephen's Day, in the UK it is – or at least was – traditionally the day for tradesmen to be given 'Christmas boxes' containing money or a present as a thank you for good service throughout the year.

According to unconfirmed sources, it has been estimated that each year around 400,000 people suffer food poisoning after eating Christmas leftovers.

Speaking of leftovers, the traditional Boxing Day feast, bubble and squeak, is the fried leftovers of the previous day's flatulence-inducing culinary excesses – Brussels sprouts, cabbage or anything else that didn't quite make it into the recycling bin, held together with a generous helping of mashed potato, usually served with a slice or two of

leftover meat on the side. Should you not feel
like frying up your Christmas Day leftovers,
supermarkets now sell both pre-prepared
frozen and tinned bubble and squeak.

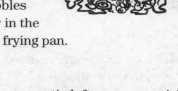

Exotic as it sounds, bubble and
squeak gained its name from the
sound it makes
as it bubbles
away in the
frying pan.

Not that you have time to fry up exotic leftovers, especially
as, since 5am, you may well have been queuing up outside a
large department store, awaiting the start of the 9am sale.

Boxing Day – the day you return unwanted presents and come
home with boxes of discounted goods. The official Twelve
Days of Christmas have barely begun but, in today's fast-
paced world, they are all but over for another nine months.

Section 9

CHRISTMAS PAST

Chapter 34

CHRISTMAS LEFTOVERS

FROM eggnog to badgers, time to delve into the Christmas leftovers…

Eggnog Riot

With alcohol possession and drunkenness prohibited, two days before Christmas 1826, cadets at the United States Military Academy in West Point, New York, smuggled rum and whisky into the North Barracks to make eggnog for a Christmas Day party. Cadets being cadets, the party began during the night of Christmas Eve, and by morning it had all got out of hand.

The party discovered, swords were drawn, firewood thrown through windows and at least one shot fired.

Although not exactly akin to the American Civil War, by coincidence one of the cadets involved in the Eggnog Riot was Jefferson Davis, later to lead the Confederacy during the American Civil War and to become the one-and-only President of the Confederate State of America.

Little Larry

Before arriving at the name of Tiny Tim, Charles Dickens considered a number of other names for his diminutive character in *A Christmas Carol*. On the shortlist were Puny Pete, Small Sam and Little Larry.

The Last Noel

In 1996, carol singers were reportedly barred from two large shopping centres in Pensacola, Florida, after shoppers complained they were both too loud and taking up too much space.

What the Heck...?

The West Yorkshire town of Heckmondwike lays claim to the UK's first public display of Christmas illuminations. The year was 1868, and the lights – said to depict everything from badgers, pigs and peacocks to elephants and a pair of boxing cats – were gas-powered.

A Great Lace to Be

Talking of lights, in 2011 the Christmas illuminations in Aylesbury were branded the shabbiest in Britain, after faulty wiring and broken bulbs left displays with Santa Claus with no face, a reindeer with a missing leg and one antler, a sign wishing shoppers 'seasns eets', and another describing the Buckinghamshire town as 'a great lace to be'.

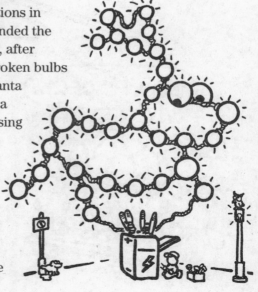

SMS

The first SMS text message was sent on 3 December 1992, by Neil Papworth, a test engineer working for the Sema Group, an Anglo-French IT services company in the UK. The message, sent to the phone of Vodafone director Richard Jarvis, read…